GOOD COMPANY

Rita F. Snowden is widely known in many countries and is the author of more than sixty books for adults and children. After six years at business she trained as a deaconess of the New Zealand Methodist Church, serving in turn two pioneer country areas before moving to the largest city for several years of social work during an economic depression.

Miss Snowden has served the world Church, beyond her own denomination, with regular broadcasting commitments. She has written and spoken in Britain, Canada, the United States, in Australia, and in Tonga at the invitation of Queen Salote. She has represented her church at the World Methodist Conference in Oxford; later being elected the first woman Vice-President of the New Zealand Methodist Church, and President of its Deaconess Association. She is an Honorary Vice-President of the New Zealand Women Writers' Society, a Fellow of the International Institute of Art and Letters, and a member of P.E.N.

Miss Snowden has been honoured by the award of the Order of the British Empire, and by the citation of "The Upper Room" in America.

Her most recent books are *Prayers for Busy People*, *Christianity Close to Life*, *Bedtime Stories and Prayers* (for children), *I Believe Here and Now*, *Discoveries That Delight*, *Further Good News* and *Continually Aware*.

GW00632163

Books by the same author
available in Fount Paperbacks

BEDTIME STORIES AND PRAYERS
(for children)
CHRISTIANITY CLOSE TO LIFE
CONTINUALLY AWARE
DISCOVERIES THAT DELIGHT
FURTHER GOOD NEWS
I BELIEVE HERE AND NOW
MORE PRAYERS FOR WOMEN
PRAYERS FOR BUSY PEOPLE
PRAYERS FOR THE FAMILY
PRAYERS IN LATER LIFE
A WOMAN'S BOOK OF PRAYERS

Rita Snowden also edited
IN THE HANDS OF GOD
by William Barclay

RITA F. SNOWDEN

GOOD COMPANY

Collins
FOUNT PAPERBACKS

First published by Fount Paperbacks, London in 1985

© 1985 by Rita F. Snowden

Made and printed in Great Britain by
William Collins Sons & Co. Ltd, Glasgow

CONDITIONS OF SALE
This book is sold subject to the condition
that it shall not, by way of trade or otherwise,
be lent, re-sold, hired out or otherwise circulated
without the publisher's prior consent in any form of
binding or cover other than that in which it is
published and without a similar condition
including this condition being imposed
on the subsequent purchaser

Dedication

Among the many special people in my
life are two doctors – husband and wife
– Dr Jean and Dr James Morehead, to
whom this book is dedicated. I love
them for their lively Christian
discipleship, their respect for persons,
and compassion in the exercise of their
ministering skills. Their footprints are
in many places.

Contents

Introduction

It is more than a coincidence that among the countless books I have carried home during the years, a number have been by doctors – autobiographies chiefly. I have found them so close to life, many of them revealing the qualities I have come to love in the lives of Dr Jean and Dr Jim.

But of all the books in my life, read and reread, foremost is that holding the superb writings of Dr Luke. There, for the first time, I found that trio: "lively discipleship, respect for persons, and compassion in the exercise of ministering skills".

Dr Luke lived to write between the years A.D. 80 and 90, when he was required to show as well a special kind of courage. Christianity was then often under attack, in ways that most of us have no experience of today. But when called to defend it, Dr Luke did not argue as "he went on his rounds" – he wrote about it. And what he then set down has fascinated readers ever since. His words – reaching us in two books, his Gospel and his Book of Acts – are really one book, both dedicated to the same distinguished person.

Over a cup of tea once in Glasgow, my good friend Dr William Barclay and I talked of this at length, and he said something that won my heart immediately: "If I had to choose to keep one book of the New Testament, and one book only, the book I would choose would be Luke's Gospel, for in it," he added, "I believe we have Jesus at His most beautiful, and the Gospel at its widest."

Then he went on to remark on the great amount that Dr Luke wrote, and a few years after that unforgettable tea-time, I found my friend setting down in one of his books a neat summing-up of our conversation that day: "In the printed Revised Standard Version of the New Testament there are five hundred and fifty-two pages. Luke's Gospel takes up seventy-eight pages; and Acts, the other book which Luke wrote, takes up seventy-one pages – that is a hundred and forty-nine pages in all." (This means that Dr Luke wrote more than Paul!)

An even more interesting fact, to me, was the number of medical terms Dr Luke used. My friend showed me where (in Luke 4:35) he reported on the man with an unclean spirit as "when the devil had thrown him" – in the very medical term for convulsions; and (in 9:38) recording the meeting of the Master with a distressed father at the foot of the mountain, saying, "I beseech Thee, look upon my son; for he is mine only child", Dr Luke uses the conventional term for a doctor visiting a patient. Even yet more striking, Dr Barclay informed me, was the word he chose to use in speaking of the camel and the needle's eye – the word *belonē*, the technical word for a surgeon's needle (Luke 18:25).

The only writer in the New Testament not a Jew, we know that Paul cherished Dr Luke, throughout hazardous years, as a fellow worker (Philemon 24). When others had departed, he remained steadfast – still with Paul whilst in prison in Rome.

For a time, I had myself been struck to find that Dr Luke is the only Gospel recorder who pauses to tell of the eighty-mile journey of Mary and Joseph, all the hot, dusty way to Bethlehem, to the census-taking, only to find the place overcrowded when at last they get there – so that there is no room for them in the Inn. Being a doctor, Luke handles the situation with great compassion and gentleness. He knows that, strictly speaking, Mary should not have been on the road at all – even riding on a donkey. But she had no choice – for they were summoned to the census-taking! Mary was coming to the close of her "nine months of womanly patience". (Dr Luke took account of all this, and set it down for us, ever afterwards. Today, where life is harsh for many within the sanctities of birth and family life, they can understand how things were within that inhospitable setting for one little One – *Who was none other than the Son of God* – placed on earth's records that census-taking.)

None of us now knows where that actual record parchment is – it would be wonderful to find it extant. But we haven't got it and perhaps it's just as well – men might even fight over it, or even worship it, as they have done over such pieces of papyrus wrested from the sands and dust-heaps of old civilizations. But we do have Dr Luke's sympathetic statement of how it happened: "It came to pass in those days," he says, "that there went out a decree from Caesar Augustus, that all the world should be taxed. (And this taxing was first made when Cyrenius was governor of Syria.) And all went to be taxed, every one into his own city. And Joseph also went up from Galilee, out of the city of Nazareth, into Judaea, unto the city of David, which is called Bethlehem (because he was of the house and lineage of David); to be taxed with Mary his espoused wife, being great with child. And so it was, that, while they were there, the days were accomplished that she should be delivered. And she brought forth her firstborn son, and wrapped him in swaddling clothes, and laid him in a manger; because there was no room for them in the inn" (Luke 2:1–7; A.V.). The newer versions (Moffatt and the Good News Bible) use the word "census", which is more meaningful to us than the Authorized Version's "tax".

One early census we do have to read through, and wonder about, in the light of Dr Luke's story, begins: "Gaius Maximus, Prefect of Egypt, orders: 'Seeing that the time has come for the house to house census, it is necessary to compel all those who, for any cause whatsoever, are residing outside their districts, to return to their own homes, that they may carry out the regular order of the census, and may also diligently attend to the cultivation of their allotments.'"

Our modern census papers – brought to our homes for us – offer instructions quite as precise. If you are "head of the house", you will read them more than likely with puckered brow. So many questions are there set to be answered – honestly – on Christian names, surnames, sex, birthplace, nationality, occupation, and on and on. One note of instruction I have long remembered, runs to the effect that if there is *a baby in the house*, still too young to be named, the "head of the house" must write in "Baby" for the Christian name. (And on the back of the form is an example to show how it must be done; so that a family return should read: "William Brown, Katherine Brown, John Brown, and 'Baby' Brown.")

This sent me back with interest to Dr Luke's report of that census-taking when there was a certain New Babe, "wrapped in swaddling clothes, and lying in a manger", of all places. But, of course, He already had a name, following on a divine injunction: "Thou shalt call His name 'Jesus'."

So, He got into the records, there and then, when "all the world was first taxed". "All the world" was hyperbole, of course, for the one mighty Roman Empire. History finds room to record that that first census raised storms of protest among the Jews, resulting in a famous insurrection in Galilee.

But in time things settled, and a census was taken at agreed intervals, requiring every citizen to supply his name and age, together with the name and age of his wife, and a statement giving the number of his children *and slaves*. The latter, fortunately, has long since fallen out of any request. Nor is one now required (as in early times) to declare the amount of one's family debt, and the names of creditors.

The scope of our now immense undertaking has been gradually sorted out. The first census in modern England (1801) showed some progress, following William the Conqueror's effort with "The Domesday Book" – which can still be seen in the Public Record Office in London.

The first census in my own country, I am told, was really a district survey, made in 1843; but it came to grief, because the Maoris killed the statistician. We have become a little more civilized since then, although, on a recent census-taking (according to the newspapers), a few door-slammers and dog-owners did repel form-deliverers. However, by the time they emerged from the Courtroom they were persuaded that it was better to co-operate.

Census-taking always, of course, where immense populations are concerned, calls for millions of forms printed on tons of paper, and the physical/practical task of collecting them again, after which they all have to be checked. Every human being in the land, at the stroke of midnight on a set date, must be accounted for!

And each question must be answered – just how many rooms are in one's house? has it a piece of garden big enough to grow potatoes? has it a piped water supply? an electric clothes-washing machine? a refrigerator? – questions that couldn't have been asked in Bethlehem, or when William the Conqueror was making his Domesday Book; or even when the first modern census was being taken in England, not to mention the first one in my own country. What it will lead to, in future census-takings, I have no idea!

One glorious reality, nevertheless, runs through them all – *each tender baby counts* – as good Dr Luke rejoiced to declare, so precious is God's gift of life! Today nameless babes must be counted, even before their eager parents can attend to this great matter of deciding between "Jean" and "Jane", and "Tom" and "Tim". And in every hospital and every nursing home, and every shelter for venerable age, someone must assume responsibility for filling in the records. Landladies must cover their boarders; hotel managers and heads of boarding-schools and colleges get busy about those under their roofs. Captains of ships, officers of airports, and guards of trains have a like duty.

No living soul must be overlooked, not even those in prison cells. And police patrols must seek out vagrants who linger in shadowy streets or scruffy parks; all must be counted, who breathe the air and know life of any sort on this earth. A surprising amount was expected, even as long ago as when Dr Luke was writing , even in those early and simple days, when Quirinius was Governor.

English Joan Bruce has given me permission, I am happy to say, to quote her poem "In the Records", which beautifully sums up Dr Luke's concern:

> In overcrowded Bethlehem
> He was born,
> among the dust and sweat
> of tired travellers
> competing for lodgings,
> with families greeting relatives
> and meeting long lost friends,
> noisily catching up on news.
> Meals were cooking,
> children crying,
> fires flickering
> as darkness fell
> in David's town
> on that unsilent night.
>
> Folk jostled, pushed and waited
> in the morning light,
> waited to comply
> with the state decree,
> the only reason for their journeying.
> His family, another number
> added to the census roll
> by form-filling civil servants.
> A statistic *in the records*. . .
> could God have been
> more down to earth than that?

Introduction

I wonder . . .
was He, later,
in the books again,
filed under crucifixion?

(Copyright)

Full of People

Seeing my typewriter on a handy table in my lounge, an elderly caller today asked whether I did all my writing there. "Oh, no!" I answered, "in fact, I have only lately moved out, to take advantage of the hot wall panel during the winter. Up till now, I've only ever had one phone – and the move has saved me a lot of running to and fro, till I can get an extension. And I'm handier here to the front doorbell, and through the opposite door, to my little kitchen. Come, I'll show you!" I led her into the study. I can only think that she had never been into a study before – her eyebrows went up, as she exclaimed at the shelves of books!

"Are you a reader?" I asked. "Do you go to the Library?" When she assured me that she did – and added, by way of compliment, that she'd read some of my books from there – I asked her: "What kind of books do you like best?" To that, her answer came: "*I like books full of people!*"

*

When now I think of her simple choice, I feel that Dr Luke's two books should be a wonderful find to her. They are so full of people! He has hardly started his Gospel than he is telling us of the birth expectation of Mary, the village maiden, mother of our Lord. How he could have got that so private story is a question that fascinates me, and I've no idea of its answer, any more than had Dr J. B. Phillips, the widely respected scholar and translator of our day. Looking back, he says: "When the event happened, *by far the most important in the history of this planet*, the facts were known to very few. Did Luke get his story from our

Lord's own mother? Did he 'interview' the old shepherds
on the hills and hear from their own lips of that strange
midnight when Heaven suddenly opened, and they were
sore afraid? Of course, we do not know for certain; and it
may well be that it was not until after the death of Mary,
that Luke felt at liberty to disclose the story of her divine
conception." There were gossips, even then, as Dr Luke
well knew, being deeply aware of people, in birth and
death, youth and age, and the whole drama of humanity.
Rooted for a time in the earth that bore them – and bears
us – they were so diverse, a pageant of weakness and
strength, laughter and tears, failure and success. Some
were beautifully fine characters, some tempted easily,
selfishly seeking their own ends, ready at a smile or a smirk
to barter the gains of years for immediate satisfaction. In
this, Dr Luke was like his Master, moving constantly
amongst people, and expecting always to be gladdened by
a wholehearted response.

> [Jesus] called out the unknown best from Peter, James,
> And all the rest, who met Him face to face,
> And lent their lives to His amazing grace
> Of humour, irony and insight; flames
> Of lambent love in Him seared out the shames
> Of life-long littleness . . . till base
> Was base no more, and even commonplace
> Became uncommon, till their names
> Grew strong to move a world that would have
> Thought them simple, stupid, ordinary men,
> As once, they had been, helpless for the task –
> Till Christ up-caught in them the gold He sought!
>
> (Anon)

Another thing that stands out is the shining consistency of
Luke's witness. Never for a moment doeshis service, or his
record, falter. The only writer in the New Testament not
a Jew, he made a unique contribution, and, as a doctor,

came close to people. Paul names him with affection, in a customary postscript to one of his letters: "Luke, the beloved physician" (Colossians 4:14; A.V.). *He seems, in a particular way, to be able to pass on the compassion that marked the Master's ministry amongst men and women.* Early in his Gospel – Luke 7:13; A.V. – he tells of His sad meeting with the widow of Nain, as she follows the bier of her only son. His words, translated, are: "And when the Lord saw her, *He had compassion* on her, and said unto her, Weep not! And He came and touched the bier; and they that bare him stood still. And He said, Young man, I say unto thee Arise!"

We get the same loving consideration in Luke's widely shared story of the Good Samaritan, who journeying, came on a poor wretch lying at the roadside, "came where he was, and when he saw him, *he had compassion on him*" (Luke 10:33; A.V.).

And Luke rejoices to underline the same quality in his story of the lost son of a loving father, returned home: "And when he was yet a great way off, his father saw him, and *had compassion*, and ran, and fell on his neck, and kissed him" (Luke 15:20; A.V.).

"All the feeling which my father could not put into words", said Dame Freya Stark, in writing a little while ago, "was in his hand – any dog, child, or horse would recognize the kindness of it." So it was, in a glorious degree, in the ministry of our gracious Master, and in Luke's recording of it.

Luke also showed unusual respect for ordinary people – for many, indeed, whom others brushed past, if they did not actually hate them. Such were the Samaritans. Again and again, Luke showed one and another of them in a good light (Luke 10:30–37; 17:11–19; A.V.). From the earliest time in which he set about his Gospel, he was at pains to say that the revelation of God was *also for the Gentiles* (Luke 2:32; A.V.). With the same grace, he mentions the widow of Zarephath – and it would be plain to many that, living where she did, she would be a Syrophoenician by race – and Naaman the leper was, of course, a Syrian; but both are graciously mentioned in the record, as people of faith (Luke 4:25–27; A.V.). And along with these, Luke makes room for a Gentile centurion, possessed of this same laudable quality (Luke 7:1–10; A.V.).

What I have already hinted at, I must here make even more sure: *Dr Luke shows a marked interest in the role of women*, in both his Gospel and in his second book, telling of the expanding pattern of the early Church. This, to early readers of his words, must then have seemed remarkable; for women were generally of little account in those times. Apart from Dr Luke's early birth stories of Jesus and His forerunner – involving Elizabeth, and Mary (Luke 1:5, 24, 25, 57, 58) – and an introduction to the aged Anna, the prophetess (Luke 2:36–38), and to the widow of Nain, burdened with grief; there is the woman who puts in an appearance in Simon's house (Luke 7:36–50; A.V.) and Mary Magdalene, who has suffered from seven devils; and Susanna; Joanna, wife of Chuza, Herod's steward, and therefore a member of high society (Luke 8:2; A.V.), and Martha and Mary, the hospitable sisters of Bethany (Luke 10:38–42; A.V.). And we must not forget "the weeping, merciful daughters of Jerusalem", at the time of the Crucifixion (Luke 23:27; A.V.).

And this well-established respect for women continues in Luke's "Book of Acts", where we meet Sapphira, wife of Ananias; Priscilla, wife of Felix; Bernice, the sister of Herod Agrippa II; Tabitha; Mary, the mother of John Mark; the maid, Rhoda; Lydia, the businesswoman of Thyatira; the slave girl whom Paul freed of "a spirit of divination"; Damaris of Athens; and the four daughters of Philip the evangelist; with a passing mention of Paul's sister in Jerusalem (Acts 23:16; A.V.): "When Paul's sister's son heard of their lying wait, he went and entered into the castle, and told Paul." A fine company of women!

Dr Luke shows himself also with a marked love for the poor. He likes to mention that his Master often found Himself in their company – and was not infrequently judged for it (Luke 14:12; 19:2–10; A.V.). Jesus consorted with many whom others passed by. He was no respecter of persons, not even a distraught thief beside Him on a cross (Luke 23:39–43; A.V.).

Using the terms "rich" and "poor", in their most literal sense, Luke also spoke out on the proper stewardship of wealth, both in his Gospel and in the Book of Acts. He reports his Lord's parables of the rich fool; of the dishonest steward; and of the rich man and poor, wretched Lazarus. And sayings of Jesus, spoken to encourage alms-giving, are just as purposefully quoted. After a first real contact with Jesus, Zacchaeus is praised for promising half his goods to feed the poor; Paul, in turn, is quoted as urging the Ephesian elders to "help the weak". Many of the Christians of those early days are remembered graciously, as having pooled their resources for distribution "to each as any had need". Barnabas, of generous spirit, is ready to share the proceeds of a piece of his land. And the deceitful husband and wife, at the other extreme, Ananias and Sapphira, who "lied to the Holy Spirit", claiming they had given their all, are shown up as a lifelong warning to everyone.

Dr Luke underlines also the vital importance and abiding presence of the Holy Spirit. (As against a mere six references to the Spirit made in Mark's Gospel, and twelve in Matthew's, there are seventeen in Luke's Gospel, and fifty-seven in the Book of Acts!)

Luke is at pains, also, to emphasize that Christianity, from its very beginning, was intended of God to be a world-wide religion – with no racial limitations at all. Issuing, as it had, from the small setting of Palestine, this was tremendous, and Luke proclaimed it with joy!

It must have given Luke great satisfaction to be able to quote a fellow worker, Peter, when writing his Book of Acts, his other book of people. His telling words, that

21

reach us now in Moffatt's translation, read: "I see quite
plainly that *God has no favourites*, but that he who
reverences Him and lives a good life in any nation is
welcomed by Him" (Acts 10:34–35). In a later passage of
the same book (17:24–28; A.V.) he sets down the stirring
words of his colleague, Paul: "God that made the world
and all things therein, seeing that He is Lord of heaven and
earth, dwelleth not in temples made with hands; neither is
worshipped with men's hands, as though He needed
anything, seeing He giveth to all life, and breath, and all
things; and *hath made of one blood all nations of men for
to dwell on all the face of the earth* . . . for in Him, we live,
and move, and have our being!"

And these glorious realities – close to Luke's heart,
bound up with the universal Gospel of God's love and
forgiveness – still await our human acceptance.

Some of us – for biological reasons more than for deeply
felt religious ones – have now come to a point where we
partly own our "togetherness". Those who give to blood
banks for the saving of life (or who receive from them)
know that the pigmentation of skin has no deep
significance. If medical science can get us to share from our
veins, what hinders us from sharing our gifts of mind and
spirit? A Britisher, travelling in the East Indies, is
protected from malaria through the service of a
Frenchman, Pasteur, and a German, Koch; a German is
protected from typhoid by the help of a Russian,
Metchnikoff; an American living in the Far East owes his
safety to a Japanese, Kitasate, who isolated the germ of
tetanus; a Russian owes his life to a blood transfusion for
which he must thank an Austrian, Landsteiner; little
children, the world round, irrespective of colour, are as
well protected from diphtheria by the research of a
Japanese and a German; are shielded from smallpox by an
Englishman: and saved from rabies by the devotion of a
Frenchman.

*

Of all the books that I have read, I can't think of any two more "full of people" than the two Dr Luke gave us; or more relevant to our peace of heart, and praise of God!

Praise, As Well As Pain

In Luke's Gospel, the phrase "Praising God" occurs oftener than in all the rest of the New Testament. This is a recent discovery to me, and I shall never now forget it. It spills over – as from a heart that cannot, in sharing, contain its praise – into "The Acts of the Apostles". But it is in the Gospel that a glorious threefold paean of praise is recorded.

Whilst visiting Jerusalem, I had an unexpected opportunity of going a few miles out, to the village birthplace of John the Baptist, forerunner of Jesus our Lord. The village lies in a wide embrace of hills, green now with olive groves. Ever since the sixth century, I learned, it has been cherished as the dwelling place of the aged Zacharias and Elizabeth (introduced in Luke 1). Both of priestly descent, as Dr Hastings was happy to remind us, the mother was a kinswoman of Mary, mother of Jesus. It was to the home of these gentle, God-fearing people, that the young Mary came for comfort and strength, on being told her surprising news by the angel visitant (Luke 1:36–40; A.V.).

A steep climb leads one today up to the Church of the Visitation. The scene of Mary's arrival at Elizabeth's home is glorified in a large mosaic on the external front of the church. And on the high wall that borders its inner court, recorded in many languages, is Mary's Praise song, *The Magnificat*, an outpouring unmatched in humble wonder and poetic utterance. Though doubtless moved by a reverent acknowledgement of a like fountain of feeling recorded of Hannah, long before, at the promise of a child (1 Samuel 1:11; A.V.), it in no way lessens the fittingness and glad beauty of Mary's own words:

24

My soul doth magnify the Lord,
And my spirit hath rejoiced in God my Saviour.
For he hath regarded the low estate of his handmaiden;
For, behold, from henceforth all generations shall call
    me blessed.
For he that is mighty hath done to me great things;
And holy is his name.
And his mercy is on them that fear him
From generation to generation.
He hath shewed strength with his arm;
He hath scattered the proud in the imagination of their
    hearts.
He hath put down the mighty from their seats,
And exalted them of low degree.
He hath filled the hungry with good things;
And the rich he hath sent empty away.
He hath holpen his servant Israel,
In remembrance of his mercy;
As he spake to our fathers,
To Abraham, and to his seed for ever!

                         (Luke 1:46–55; A.V.)

A praiseful, revolutionary song, it is still, to this day, sung
in the world Church of Mary's Son, our Lord!

*

In the same early chapter of his Gospel, Luke records *The
Benedictus*, the song of the old man, Zacharias, chosen of
God to be the father of John the Baptist, forerunner of the
Son of God. And that song, too, is still sung within the
Christian Church. Ordinarily, an elderly singer might be
stirred to praise of God solely by a sense of patriotism, or
of material benefits; but old Zacharias is lifted up by
consideration of spiritual realities. His song is:

Blessed be the Lord God of Israel;
For he hath visited and redeemed his people,
And hath raised up an horn of salvation for us
In the house of his servant David;
As he spake by the mouth of his holy prophets, which
 have been since the world began:
That we should be saved from our enemies, and from the
 hand of all that hate us;
To perform the mercy promised to our fathers,
And to remember his holy covenant;
The oath which he sware to our father Abraham,
That he would grant unto us, that we, being delivered
 out of the hand of our enemies
Might serve him without fear,
In holiness and righteousness before him, all the days of
 our life.
And thou, child, shalt be called the prophet of the
 Highest:
For thou shalt go before the face of the Lord to prepare
 his ways;
To give knowledge of salvation unto his people
By the remission of their sins.
Through the tender mercy of our God;
Whereby the dayspring from on high hath visited us,
To give light to them that sit in darkness and in the
 shadow of death,
To guide our feet into the way of peace!

(Luke 1:68–79; A.V.)

*

And the threefold paean of praise is completed in Dr
Luke's next chapter under the title: *The Nunc Dimittis*. The
promised Son of God, to be named JESUS, *has been born*;
and His earth-parents, Mary and Joseph, have brought
Him to the Temple – as required of the Law – and as an
offering, a pair of turtle doves instead of a lamb because
they are poor. And at that moment of entry, devout old

Simeon, who has long treasured a promise that he should
not know death until he has seen God's promise fulfilled,
appears. And taking the Child into his arms, he bursts into
praise:

> Lord, now lettest thou thy servant depart in peace,
> According to thy word:
> For mine eyes have seen thy salvation,
> Which thou hast prepared before the face of all people;
> A light to lighten the Gentiles,
> And the glory of thy people Israel.
>
> (Luke 2:29–32)

*

But Luke, the recorder, finds that he must go on, and
straightway goes on (in what is now translated as his next
chapter) to tell of "the multitude of the heavenly host
praising God" (2:13; A.V.). Then he reports "the
shepherds returning, *praising God* for all things" (2:20;
A.V.). And with so much to record of the rich years of his
Master's ministry, Luke goes on to His post-Crucifixion
days, to a great praiseful occasion some time beyond His
Resurrection, that no Christian should ever forget: "He led
them out as far as to Bethany, and e lifted up is hands, and
blessed them. And it came to pass, while he blessed them,
he was parted from them, and carried up into heaven. And
they worshipped him, and returned to Jerusalem with great
joy; and were continually in the Temple, *praising and
blessing God*" (24:50–53; A.V.).

*

Now, with his Gospel at an end, devoted Dr Luke leaps as
eagerly into his "Acts of the Apostles", to say, after a
passage of time, "And they, continuing daily with one
accord in the Temple, and breaking bread from house to
house, did eat their meat with gladness and singleness of
heart *praising God*" (2:46–47; A.V.).

27

But that isn't all, wonderful as it is, that ongoing pattern of praise! Soon, Peter and John, about the service of their Risen and Ascended Lord, as they go up to the Temple to offer their praise, find themselves ministering to a poor fellow, lame and helpless, carried daily and set down at the gate called "Beautiful". But when he begs alms of them, Peter's unexpected answer is: "Silver and gold have I none; but such as I have, I give thee; 'In the name of Jesus Christ of Nazareth, rise up and walk!'" What an unexpected gift that was! And what a joy it must have been later to Dr Luke to set it in his "Acts of the Apostles". Their Master and Lord was no longer with His disciples in bodily form – *but His healing power was still gloriously adequate*! For it was nothing but the truth to say, of him who had for so long been carried to beg: "He leaping up stood, and walked and entered with them into the Temple, walking and leaping, *and praising God*!"

*

So the close friends of the Risen Christ were on their way to become His Church – the way of *Service and Praise*!

And centuries passed.

Til in one, no great time before our own, in fact, as near as the Early Methodists in their Conference of 1791, when the customary question was asked: "Who have died this year?" the triumphant response came: "Wyatt Andrews – who died full of Faith and the Holy Ghost. As long as he could ride, he travelled, and *while he had breath he praised God*!"

Is there anything surer than that? It would have rejoiced the heart of Dr Luke to be able to add that to his "Acts of the Apostles". And I can imagine nothing lovelier, than that it might be said of you and me – Christians today, possessed of a quicker means of covering the miles than on horseback – that we *are possessed by the same unvarying praise*!

Meanwhile, till our breath is spent, there is inspiration in Dr Luke's record of Mary's *Magnificat*, Zacharias's

Benedictus, and in old Simeon's *Nunc Dimittis*, not forgetting the paean of praise rising from the life service of others up through the changing years, until this day. Many have left us, as well, inspiration in their hymns of praise – our hymnbooks are rich. One has only to cast an eye down the index, to fasten on the ageless word "Praise" again and again repeated. When I came, not long ago, to seek a hymn for a shared Service following the death of my dear friend Rene, there were many to choose from. I chose the one she had herself marked in the back of her hymnbook:

> Praise, my soul, the King of heaven,
>   To His feet thy tribute bring;
> Ransomed, healed, restored, forgiven,
>   Who like thee, His praise should sing?
>   Praise Him! Praise Him!
>   Praise Him! Praise Him!
> Praise the everlasting King!
>   (Henry Francis Lyte, 1793–1847)

We did!

And my heart was lifted up in giving praise to God, for my friend, at the surrender of her "daily breath". In a favourite collection of things I've been looking at again, is Ernest Raymond's tribute at the passing of a close friend, a fellow author. He wrote as feelingly: "I can offer no greater tribute to the quality of Pamela Frankau as a human being, than to say that when word came that she was dead my immediate feeling was a sudden unforeseen heightening of my belief (or if belief is too strong a word, my hope) of human immortality . . . I do not think that this sudden surge of faith . . . was a mere 'wish fulfilment'. Such an easy emotion would have been unworthy of Pamela. It was just that I felt it intellectually impossible to believe that the splendid intelligence, the keen and eager vision, the large, loving, laughing heart which was Pamela, would cease to be. To believe that anything so brilliant, so shining with a glow that surely came from the very stuff of Reality, would have suddenly become nothing, seemed analogous, in a small way, to supposing that the sun is not still there, because night has intervened . . . The last words of her Will, written when she believed that death was near, are, '*I give praise and thanks to Almighty God for the gift of life*. I thank my loves, my friends, my acquaintances, and my benefactors, for helping to make it such a good adventure.'"

So much, is worth such praise!

Growing Gladly

I was up early, it was such a lively morning! The first thing was to check the time, then put on the kettle for a cup of tea. As I stood enjoying it, the sun came in through my window. Outside, at that very moment, a blackbird high on a neighbour's tree started his matins. Inside, my attention was directed to a little handful of buds showing on a flowering pot-plant lately given me. Gladness was the mood of everything – gladness associated with *growth*! And there's nothing like it. Ruskin said: "God has lent us the earth for our life!" The great thing, of course, is not to hold back! Parents, doctors, aunts and uncles anywhere who are worth the glory of their status, are interested in *growth*!

And of course Dr Luke was, for one of his loveliest verses (Luke 2:52; N.E.B.) is bursting with praise for it! From the beginning, naturally, as a doctor, he was happy to write of the birth of the Child Jesus. But he did not stop with His babyhood, as many people, even today, seem to do, being only aware of Him at Christmas, the festival of His birth. And this is a great pity!

Early, of course, He was whisked away by Joseph and Mary, as a little refugee, into Egypt – out of the way of Herod. In time, when Herod died, by the same divine direction the little family returned and settled in Nazareth.

Their next journey together was when the boy was twelve, when they travelled for several days up to Jerusalem, the Holy City, for the Feast. It was springtime, and Passover, the most important festival of the year. For weeks families had been planning the journey, together with relations and neighbours. Even family donkeys, with their saddles and traces adjusted, sensed the excitement in the air. For weeks everybody had been busy – fitting new sandals, each person cutting a stick for the journey, fitting new clothes, which must have been especially important for the twelve-year-old. He was now a sturdy lad, and the sleeves of the garments He had worn in the village, and about the hills as He ran in the sweet wind with His friends, must have been ready for replacement.

The caravan, despite a measure of tiredness, by the end of the day was a joyful company with young and old singing the ancient songs of their people, to the music of the timbrel and the flute.

Each new day found them early astir, until, at last, came the long-talked-of moment when the Holy City itself burst into view! They were footsore, and dusty – but how little it mattered! By sundown they had pitched camp on the Mount of Olives. Just across the ravine of the Kedron, no distance now, were the gleaming outlines of the Temple! The journey was behind them – and one Lad of twelve surely found it hard to settle to sleep that night!

The next days were full of interest, wonder and, in the end, concern for His parents when it was time to be well on their way home. The truth was, He became lost. From one friendly group to another, Joseph and Mary made their anxious enquiries, but nowhere could they find Him. One friend suggested one thing, one another – perhaps He had not seen them leave? Perhaps, suggested yet another, He had joined the wrong caravan, and was at that moment miles off in the wrong direction?

But no, it was none of these things. It had been understood that the young people would mingle freely, and Jesus could have been almost anywhere, but when night-time came, and their twelve-year-old did not appear, deep anxiety laid hold of His parents. The thing to do, it seemed to Joseph and Mary, was to go back to where they had last seen Him. And that was away back in the Holy City itself.

Much time passed. And there – with enormous relief – they found Him. He was in the Temple itself, listening to

the learned doctors of the Law, and asking them questions!
Oh, such relief! Such relief!

Soon they were safely together, on their way to
Nazareth, back to the familiar, the "commonplace" – home!

"His mother", wrote Dr Luke, with gentle
understanding, "treasured all these things in her heart."
Presently, there was something quite as important to add:
"*Jesus grew . . . in body and in wisdom, gaining favour with
God and men*" (Luke 2:52; Good News Bible). That was
physically, mentally, spiritually, socially!

He grew in body – as did every natural, healthy, happy
youth. Soon His caring mother, Mary, would have need to
look to His clothes once more – the sleeves, and the length
of His garments – for He was still growing and would, until
He reached the fullness of manhood. As He helped Joseph
the carpenter with hard, physical labour, His muscles
developed, His strong back took more and more strain. A
landmark in little Nazareth today, I discovered, to my great
interest, is a building called *The Church of Jesus
Adolescent*. Fittingly, it nowadays belongs to a school for
boys, and above the altar is a figure of the growing youth,
Jesus. I spent a good deal of time in little Nazareth, and
accepted an opportunity to seek out a carpenter's
workshop. It couldn't have been very different from that
in which Joseph, the village carpenter, worked at a steady
craft, long hours, with simple tools – passing on to his
young apprentice the skills that the years had taught him.
It was, for that young apprentice, still a growing time. The
poet Edward Hilton Young, pondering what it must have
meant, set down these words:

> I think, at Golgotha,
> As Jesu's eyes were closed in death,
> They saw with love most passionate
>   the village street of Nazareth.

Maybe! Memories of growing up are precious when they

have been good in actuality. Though the Master did not live, in a physical, human sense, to the age many of us know today; whilst He was in Nazareth, *He grew in body!* And Dr Luke found it good to remind us of that – *part of His fourfold growth!*

> He learned as other children learn –
> That knives are sharp, and fire will burn,
> He learned to talk, then sing a song,
> Learned right from left, and right from wrong.
> One day He would be wise and good,
> But this took time, as well it should,
> He did not want it sooner than
> The time it took to be a man.

> (Anon)

*

For Dr Luke went on to remind us that He also grew "*in wisdom*" – that meant in mental capacity, knowledge, wise judgement, with the power to apply these critically and practically, in such situations as life might throw up. (It is difficult to analyse "wisdom", but in the growth of Jesus we have records of His contact with people, and of His teaching, to turn to. These were not of His own writing, of course – He never wrote anything of that nature. The only time we read of Him writing, it was not with an equivalent of our pen or pencil, but with a finger. "The scribes and Pharisees brought unto Him a woman taken in adultery; and when they had set her in the midst, they said unto Him, Master, this woman was taken in adultery, in the very act. Now Moses in the law commanded us, that such should be stoned; but what sayest Thou? This they said, tempting Him, that they might have to accuse Him. *But Jesus stooped down, and with His finger wrote on the ground, as though He heard them not.* So when they continued asking Him, He lifted up Himself, and said unto them: He that is without sin among you, let him first cast a stone at her.

And again He stooped down, and wrote on the ground. And they which heard it, being convicted by their own conscience, went out one by one, beginning at the eldest, even unto the last: and Jesus was left alone, and the woman standing in the midst. When Jesus had lifted up Himself, and saw none but the woman, He said unto her, Woman, where are those thine accusers? Hath no man condemned thee? She said, No man, Lord. And Jesus said unto her, Neither do I condemn thee: go, and sin no more" (John 8:3–11; A.V.).

Now that, surely, is a showing of wisdom – compassionate wisdom, as all true wisdom ought to be – not a hard, heartless thing.

*

And in favour with God He grew – that is, *spiritually*. Not only in body and mind, but along with them His spirit grew. "Christians ought to be alert to differing responsibilities that God asks of different generations", said Dr Kenneth Slack, interviewed in London a while ago. In short, we ought to *grow in spirit*! "Grow" was a word continually on Paul's lips – Dr Luke must have heard him use it collectively and individually, amongst the early Christians. Ephesians 4:14–15, in the New English Bible, holds such beauty and challenge: "*We are no longer to be children* . . . No, let us speak the truth in love; so shall we *fully grow up into Christ*." In 2 Peter 3:18, in the same Version, is underlined the same lively concern for spiritual growth: "*Grow* in the grace and in the knowledge of our Lord and Saviour Jesus Christ!"

I know several long-time Christians, now up into their seventies, who want to sing the same hymns, and read the same Bible passages as they did in childhood or soon afterwards, when they claim each had an experience of "conversion". But their desires distress me, just as they would distress Paul and Luke. Two of them are retired farmers, pastoralists, long watching their undulating acres of grass grow season by season, to serve their flocks and herds. Yet, somehow, the importance of growth in the realm of the spirit does not occur to them. Another is a grandmother, with children and grandchildren behind her, and she cares for their growth; yet she still prays as her own bedtime prayer, she tells me, "Gentle Jesus, meek and mild . . ." the prayer of a young child! It's more than I can understand. Faith can't be a very vital thing to them now, though it may have been once. A more telling prayer for each of us, as we come up through the years, could be:

> O that I may *grow*!
> I see the leaves out-pushing hour by hour;
> With steady joy the buds burst into flower,
> Urged gladly on by Nature's waking power;
>   *O that I may grow!*

(Anon)

*

But even this prayer needs to embrace other people; we must go on *to grow in all our human relationships!* Jesus did! But it isn't easy, surrounded as our lives are with so many persons, and all so different! The first secret is to meet them *with respect*, as Jesus did! Said Dame Edith Evans, in our day, "*People are people, wherever you meet them!*" And this was what she meant. There aren't any of them whom we meet here who are just cardboard characters – they are people, with long hopes, and fears, and human frailties, and strong acts of courage, like ourselves – men and women, of all ages and nationalities! Parents they are, some of them, builders, artists, counsellors, saints, failures, successes. Some spill the gold of laughter and the bracing support of friendship in lonely places; some reach out a hand when help of another kind is needed.

Despite travel in outer space, you and I meanwhile belong with these earth people. Our challenge is *to establish a relationship with them*, as being God's people. Some of them fail to recognize this relationship – but does it make any difference to us? Someone lately presented his query to a great national newspaper editor: "Will we", he asked, "be happier for seeing the other side of the Moon, or strolling in the meadows of Mars?" The answer that came was a very Christ-like answer: *"The greatest adventure of all, is not to go to the Moon . . . It is rather to understand the heart and soul of man, and to turn away from wrath and destruction towards creativeness and brotherly love!"*

In Our Wildernesses

A short way from my front door is a turn which takes my feet past a fascinating shopwindow. It shows ships with tall sails set, and tiny cars, trains, and bright cardboard boxes that hold other treasures. I've never seen any dolls there – though a favourite story of temptation, passed on by Kenneth Grahame, of *The Wind in the Willows* fame, centres on them. It was one of two children, who stood pressing eager eyes and noses against such a shopwindow, who first spoke of it. "I know what she wants most", said Harold. "She wants that set of tea things . . . with the red and blue flowers on 'em; she's wanted it for months, 'cos her dolls are getting big enough to have real afternoon tea, and she wants it so badly that she won't walk that side of the street, when we go into town. *But it costs five shillings!*"

That, of course, is a good way to handle temptation: *not deliberately to "walk into it"*. But there are times when one has no preliminary choice. It comes so suddenly and so unexpectedly!

Another thing that must be understood about temptation – before one can think sensibly about it, or help another with it – is that temptation, in itself, is not sin.

More than this: it may come from without, but *it must be settled from within*. It takes many forms – and is usually fashioned of something highly desirable, not a bad thing in itself. (It might be a dolls' tea set; it might be a plane ride. Eric Gill, world famous English sculptor and typographer, is remembered as having said during his first flight: "I can't tell you how nice it is – it is nice enough *to be a temptation*." That's an important point!)

Jesus discovered that, and knowing it in the deep places of His experience, felt it was something that He ought to

share with His disciples in their growing up into leadership.
If He had chosen to keep it to Himself no one would ever
have known, for it was a solitary experience. But having
told it to His disciples it has come down to us, as what Dr
William Barclay, a fellow disciple of our day, calls "a very
sacred story; for it can have come from no other source
than His own lips". In time, of course, Dr Luke wrote it
into his Gospel (Luke 4:1–13; A.V.). Of all that appears
there – the gift of our Lord, concerning the complex
business of living – scarcely anything can be more valuable
to us. For temptation is part of human experience on this
earth of men and women – even Jesus had to know that.
And as it comes to many a one at a particularly significant
time of life, so it came to Him, setting out into His life
ministry. Though Dr Luke is anxious to have us understand
that it didn't, once and for all, end there (v. 13; A.V.). The
tempter, he tells us, "departed from Him for a season", or
as the Revised Standard Version puts it, "until an
opportune time". There is no solitary temptation, any
more than there is an "instant", or "easy" victory over
temptation. When the Master returned after forty days,
from His initial experience in the Wilderness, it was a
threefold temptation of which He had to tell His disciples,
but it was not all. As life went on, it appeared again and
again – though never in the same form – when the crowd
would crown Him King, after they had found that He could
feed them with bread, a material gift, and He was thus a
good kind of king to have. And there were other occasions,
not least in the exacting experience in the Garden of
Gethsemane. And He was even challenged by "sight-
seers" to come down from His Cross!

These days we are all in such a hurry, it is hard for us to
accept the fact that temptation is sometimes a sustained
siege. We want what we have to do, done; we have our
"Instant coffee", our "Instant gravy", our "Instant
pudding".

But temptation, we discover, seldom returns in the

same guise (or we would be ready for it), and never in the guise in which it came to our Young Master. "Ours is no temptation", as Dr William Barclay reminds us, "to turn stones into bread, or leap from a Temple pinnacle, for the simple reason that to us it is impossible. These are temptations which could only have come to a man whose powers were unique, and who had to decide how to use them." The curious thing is that temptation is so often compounded of perfectly good things, as Dr W. R. Maltby, to whom we owe much illumination, wrote in his beautiful little book *The Significance of Jesus*. "His temptations", he had to underline for us, "were not those which come to a base or an ambitious or a presumptuous nature. They found Him on the side where He was most vulnerable – on the side of compassion. *Food so hard to find, justice so hard to come by, God so hard to know* – it was the woes of the world which called to that mighty heart, and He found it hard to withhold."

*

His first temptation there in the Wilderness was understandably, occasioned by His own desperate hunger, to embrace the need of the hungry masses, and turn stones into bread. Aggravated by the very setting in which He found Himself, it was the more desperate. A young man, and alone, after forty days in that bare, uninhabited place of some fifteen by thirty-five miles, reaching down towards the Dead Sea, one is not surprised that it happened. Nor was Dr Luke, when he came to record it, in words that have been translated for us: "For days He did eat nothing, and when they were ended, He afterward hungered." It was, no doubt, a good place for contemplation and prayer – to consider, at the very start of His public ministry, what values He would set uppermost in His Kingdom, and how He would most tellingly use His new powers. The Wilderness itself was no sandy stretch, but formed of a base of limestone, and here and there loose lumps with something of the shape of loaves. In the circumstances, they made a very powerful suggestion. "And the devil" (wrote Luke in chapter 4, verses 1–4; A.V.) "said unto Him, 'If thou be the Son of God, command this stone that it be made bread.'" *If?* How often this little word is made a handy vehicle of doubt in temptation! But Jesus had no doubt, and His answer came: "It is written" – relying on the long-learned scriptures – "that man shall not live by bread alone, but by every word of God."

"Surely", some have since said, as Dr J. S. Stewart has reminded us, "if Jesus were the Son of God, He must always have done the right thing without any struggles at all. The very possibility of inward conflict is excluded. But is it? It may be glorifying Jesus to say He won His victory always without effort. But surely, it is glorifying Him far more to say He marched to it through an agony of sweat and blood. And indeed, the whole Gospel and our own hopes of salvation are bound up with a Christ Who was 'tempted in all points' – not just here and there, but in all points – 'like as we are' (Hebrews 4:15; A.V.). The dramatic story of it", adds Dr Stewart, "is told in a pictorial, symbolical way; but what we have to remember is that the experience itself was wholly inward. As we see Jesus then, we see Him not with any great, gaunt, black-winged Satan beside Him . . . not that at all; we see Jesus quite alone, sitting on a spur of rock, with His head bowed and His hands clenched, and then falling down on His knees, and then on His face, with a cry breaking from Him that sounds like: 'O God, if it be possible, let this cup pass'; and then turn our eyes away, for it is an awful thing to see the Son of God like that." How often, still, that temptation comes to leaders of men and women on earth: "If you would have them honour your God, give them *material* and not just *spiritual* gifts!"

But – as with our Lord, this has to be kept in balance!

Then comes a second temptation – the temptation of wide appeal. Jesus was allowed to see Himself taken "up into a high mountain", into a place with all the world taking notice of Him! This, I fully believe, is one temptation which, while missing most of those in the pews, comes with subtle persuasiveness, to their minister in the pulpit. It is there every time that his congregation, going out, shake him by the hand and thank him warmly for his fine preaching. (And I happen to know that it comes as subtly to a visiting woman preacher and lecturer. Have I not been guest in many places the world round? And striving ever, to offer what I believe is my very best?)

The only fitting prayer for us, in the pulpit, or in the pew, is "Lead us not into temptation". For there are no "high places" on this earth where temptation does not come. A suitable hymn verse for any Christian anywhere, may ever be:

> The Kingdom that I seek
> Is Thine; so let the way
> That leads to it be Thine!
> (Horatius Bonar)

I felt this spirit implicit in all the preaching and lecturing of the beloved Dr Herbert Farmer, when he came to our city from his "high place" in Cambridge. But he had clearly girded his spirit to meet such temptations, as many of us know when we go speaking abroad. I knew its subtlety before ever I found the Doctor writing in his book *The Servant of the Word*: "We are sincerely aware of God and His call, but we are also, when we go into the pulpit, very conscious of ourselves being aware of God and His call. We are like those tiresome people who do genuinely admire the sunset, but when they speak of it you know at once that, in addition, they admire themselves admiring the sunset."

Jesus found Himself able to resist these temptations – *but there was a third*. He found Himself, in suggestion, lifted on to the lofty pinnacle of the Temple, in the Holy City. It was suggested that He should throw Himself down – as a sensational exhibition of how God would protect Him. Everyone then living in Jerusalem, or journeying there year by year for the Feast, as Jesus Himself had done, beginning as a lad of twelve, knew that there was a sheer drop into the Kedron Valley below. But Jesus resisted the suggestion that He should win followers by any such sensation – bypassing their God-given powers of mind and will. Several times later in His ministry, Jesus would have to lose a very likely follower, rather than gain him unworthily. He sent several off back home, to think out soberly their choice. Among such people, was that very desirable young man, "the rich young ruler" of whom Dr Luke felt he had to say "And he went away sorrowful" (Luke 18:18–23; A.V.).

And to this very hour, this is the Christ Whom we serve!

So Very Vague

Every time the phone rings, or the mail comes, I rise eagerly to attend to these servants of my life. Sometimes, it is true, they lay burdens upon me; but at other times, a gift of joy, or even a chuckle. So it was lately.

Away from my typewriter for a moment, about some domestic task in my flat, the phone's imperative voice reached me. As I took up the receiver, an unknown male voice asked: "Is that Mrs Snowden?" "Miss Snowden", I answered him. "Miss Snowden," he went on, "this is the Central Post Office. We have here an overseas item of mail for you, addressed rather vaguely. Where exactly are you?" I gave him my address. "Thank you," he finished, "I will write that down – and you will get it in the morning." And I did!

Written neatly, in a bold hand across a large envelope, it had set off addressed to: "Miss Rita Snowden – Authoress, Flat –, Near Harbour Bridge, Auckland, New Zealand." For the benefit of those many friends who have not visited Auckland, I have to say it is the largest city in the land, with all the traffic, shops, business concerns, and tall-rising buildings of a city, linked by our eight-laned arching Bridge, carrying thousands continually to another, but lesser city by the sea, where I live. And the vision of an author's flat, set solitarily there amid the trees and bushes, is more than "rather vague", as the Postal Officer suggested. Those of us living here – or visiting here – cannot but chuckle.

On the phone this morning, I shared it with church friends in the pew in front of me, the Rev. Harry Voyce and his wife, missionaries from the British Solomon Islands retired after a long life of outstanding service. And we chuckled together. I knew he had a story about vagueness, too, being a letter sent to his father, when he stayed with them once, in Bougainville in the Islands. "Yes," he answered me, knowing that I had voyaged several times in those mighty southern seas, "his letter came addressed, simply: '*Mr H. W. Voyce, The Pacific.*'"

For the benefit of those who haven't studied the southern map, as many of us have, since Dr Fitchett drew our attention to the fact that "this romantic, dangerous Pacific exceeds in area all the dry land in the world. Here, one might pour – had one the magic power – every drop of three Atlantics, or if one chose, seventy Mediterraneans. In the Pacific, of stirring tales, are tens of thousands of islands, ranging in size from the world's largest, New Guinea and Borneo, down to mere dots of palm-covered coral." It is not surprising if our approach to the Pacific be coloured by wide dreams of youth when we lay in the long grass reading *Kidnapped* and *Treasure Island*. In these parts, it is all too easy to be vaguely mixed up with the ferocity of the brown man, and the devilry of the white man, aided by his muskets and barter, and the more recent accomplishments of missionary men and women, like the Voyces, of glorious Christian spirit. What a modern "Acts of the Apostles" Dr Luke could have given us from this part of the world, then completely unknown. And you can be sure that there would have been nothing more vague about the triumph of Christ in the lives of men and women in the Pacific, than in his own first-century New Testament Book of Acts. Luke, as a medical man, couldn't afford to be vague – any more than a modern missionary can. He had already established that essential clarity, in writing his Gospel record. An example that readily springs to mind was the time when the Master's first disciples had to take a message of assurance to John the Baptist, during a moment of uncertainty in his dungeon prison. Immediately, we see that there was nothing in the least vague about it. He wrote: "Then Jesus, answering, said unto them, *Go your*

45

*way, and tell John what things ye have seen and heard; how
the blind see, the lame walk, the lepers are cleansed, the deaf
hear, the dead are raised, to the poor the gospel is preached.
And blessed is he, whosoever shall not be offended in me"*
(Luke 7:22–23; A.V.).

Jesus was not a vague Master – and Luke, His devoted
follower, was not a vague servant! Both his two books
reflect this shining reality: so clear, so purposeful they are,
so easily understood!

And there is no room for vagueness in the witness of any
man or woman who follows the same Master, to this day
– as missionary, or in whatever vocation he or she
embraces. This was first underlined for me by Mary Webb,
when I was growing up, speaking of one of her characters,
Amber Dark, in *The House in Dormer Forest*. "Amber's
ideas of God", she wrote, "were vague and shadowy. The
moment she tried to materialize them they vanished." I
can't help feeling that it has been the same sort of
vagueness that has held back the joy and witness of many
another Christian of my day, whom I've come to know.
One, a little more honest than some, has said so:

> I'm a Christian in my way;
> How, it's difficult to say.
> I've the haziest sort of notion
> What I mean by my devotion.
> Clichés clutter up my head,
> Catchwords are my daily bread;
> Exquisitely undefined
> Is the thing I call my mind.
>
> (Anon)

These are the sort of people who, when you speak to them
of God, say, "Yes", they believe "there is a summat
somewhere", but never get clearer or closer than that.
These are they who never once take themselves off to a
study group, or to buy themselves a simple paperback on

the Christian faith. And there are any number of us Christian writers, who devote a large part of our lives to the task of setting down joyously and clearly, the deep discoveries that we have made. There are many around us – even, occasionally, in church pews, when there is a festival of some sort: Christmas, or Easter, or a family wedding, or a baptism – who need to hear from someone they respect the kind of word that Dr J. S. Whale, President of Chestnut College, wrote: "You can no more banish clear and formulated thinking from religion," said he, "than you can from engineering, medicine, or law." I would say, "from good child-care, music, or gardening".

It was said of one modern Christian: "He was a great lover of God, *with his mind!*" A lovely tribute that I wish we could all earn – a thoroughly Christian tribute! He had, of course, a great mind! And all seeking to find the Christian way in the world benefited from it. But, it was said as truly of another, at the same time: "She hadn't a great mind – but a small mind in faithful activity!"

I feel sure Dr Luke found it a sensible, reasonable thing to report the Master's words to a certain questioner who stood up and tempted Him, saying, "Master, what shall I do to inherit eternal life?" He said unto him, "What is written in the Law? How readest thou?"

And he answering said, "Thou shalt love the Lord thy God with all thy heart, and with all thy soul, and with all thy strength, *and with all thy mind*" (Luke 10:25–27; A.V.). And one can't start too early to understand this, as my headmistress friend, Lilian Cox, said beautifully:

> To think the long, long thoughts of youth,
>   Nor be afraid of heresy;
> And yet to think those thoughts with Him,
>   And keep unstained my loyalty!

Luke was much in the company of Paul – even to the end of the way. Did he hear him say, I wonder, what he wrote so eagerly to his friends, as the most important thing he could say, at the moment? "be not conformed to this world: *but be ye transformed by the renewing of your mind*, that ye may prove what is that good, and acceptable, and perfect, will of God" (Romans 12:2; A.V.). In his widely welcomed *Letters to Young Churches*, Dr J. B. Phillips translated Paul's lively words into the language of our day: "Don't let the world around you squeeze you into its own mould, but let God remould your minds from within, so that you may prove in practice that the plan of God for you is good, meets all His demands *and moves towards the goal of true maturity*." That brings us the all-important vision of *growth* in thinking, as well as the evasion of vagueness.

We are challenged as Christians, not only to think clearly about our faith and witness in the world, right here, right now, but to put it clearly and tellingly into the language we all share. Dr David H. C. Read, in his little book *The Communication of the Gospel*, that should concern us all, is thinking especially of ministers, lay preachers and class leaders, when he says very pointedly: "If you speak to a congregation about 'the biblical paradox of man's radical sinfulness in the context of redeeming grace', you must interpret the yawns in the pew in terms of bewilderment of mind rather than hardness of heart."

God forgive us, that ever we resort to vagueness – however we do it!

Hid in Our Hands

Along with my little golden-haired twin sister, I can't
remember a time when it wasn't a joy to make things. We
had very little money, but it didn't matter. Our parents
taught us to rejoice in the secret skills hid in our hands.

In what leisure our farm afforded him, our father made
us bubble-pipes, from a large bamboo growing at the end
of the garden; and he made us each a little stool, that could
be carried into the sunshine or wherever we elected to play.
And that was not all – each season, the year round, brought
its surprises: whistles, when the willows were green; a billy-
cart from a grocer's box, with an axle and pair of wooden
wheels. Summer brought us a swing, with a carefully
smoothed seat, hanging at just the right height, under a
great tree.

I preserved, complete and unquestioning for a long time,
a delight in my father's skills with simple tools and a
pocket-knife, until, one wet afternoon indoors, I begged
him to make me a set of doll's teeth from a piece of knotted
firewood. I can still feel the jolt of that moment, when he
had to confess that my request was beyond him. I had never
imagined that anything was beyond what my father's clever
hands could do.

Happily he had other powers – he knew the calls of birds,
and could find their nests and lift me up to look in upon sky-
blue eggs, or on slightly bigger speckled ones, when the
nests were near enough to the ground. And when the
Chinese greengrocer, who gardened nearby, brought us a
caddy of China tea for Christmas – and my father and I
were the only two who liked it – I found that it wasn't only
a mother who could make a cup of tea. Soon, I had
captured all these skills I so admired. I made little ships that

49

could actually sail in the horse's drinking-trough, or in the
stream at the end of the cow-paddock, when I had adult
company to make sure I didn't fall in.

Our mother made things, too: clothes for us children,
aided by her old Singer sewing machine; garden plots of
flowers; and golden crusty bread that smelled good when
it came from her oven; butter the colour of sunshine; and
pies and cakes. One of my earliest schoolgoing memories
is of a first tiny applepie – made, I now suspect, from a bit
of pastry left over. It was in the smallest dish I'd ever seen,
and I took it to school, carrying it gently – a copy of our
big Sunday dinner pie. Mid-morning that day, at my school
desk, I could wait no longer and held up my hand to attract
the teacher's attention: "Please, Miss, may I leave the
room?" In a moment I was out. But I had no thought for
the modest pink building with one door at the end of the
playground. None at all! I hurried no further than the
Cloakroom, and to my bag hanging there – to peep in to
see whether my little pie was still safe! An hour later, when
eleven o'clock Playtime came, I peeped in a second time.
It was yet a long wait to midday lunchtime, when I might
take it out and eat it!

Growing – though without being too tomboyish – I got
a pocket-knife of my own. And learned from my father
how to make some of the things he made, entering the
best of them in the junior section of the village exhibition,
year by year. And when my Sunday School needed money
for Missions, I made and sold wooden jam-making spoons,
at sixpence a time. And there are still some in use, as I
learned to my surprise half a lifetime later, when the
Methodist Church of New Zealand honoured me as its *first*
woman Vice-President, and I returned to speak in the
village, as part of my country-wide itinerary! Each modest
spoon, thanks to my father's guidance, was made from a
particular *tasteless* New Zealand wood from which,
ordinarily, boxes were made for our overseas butter
market!

Little wonder that hands – my own, and other people's leading to craftsmanship – have been a pleasure to me all my life!

Midway in my long-time ministry as an author, with books circling the earth, I wrote and illustrated a devotional book, with the title *A Show of Hands*. I spent a long time, after I had written it, assembling beautiful, meaningful pictures from the ends of the earth, and loved doing it. Fittingly, my Preface opened with the words: "The first sight of my own hands has slipped from memory. It seems, they didn't surprise me then – but they do now." (Unhappily, the book is no longer in print.) Only that once, among many books, did it occur to me to bypass the customary habit of inserting the author's photograph, and a brief biographical note, and use instead, on the back inside slip of the dustjacket, a colour picture of the author's hands, which I got a photographer friend to supply. And beneath it, to complete my plan, my London editor, from notes supplied, made the following sketch:

"As a country child's, these hands fed hens, brought in wood, and helped in fields and orchards at harvest time. Later, as the hands of a student, they knew the feel of books and pen. Acquiring new skills, with the years, they tended the sick, closed the eyes of the dead (on district-nursing service), kindled wood fires, painted pictures, made pottery, and wrestled with motorcycles, cars, van-and-caravan. They typed letters, and books, painted house walls, laid crazy-paving, pulled weeds, mended shoes, carried bags on and off ships, planes, trains and buses the world round. They have been used on countless platforms to stress a point. Strong, practical, artistic, seldom idle, they are little different from a million others . . . but a great joy to possess and use."

A great many monotonous tasks, of course, can be turned over to machines in these days of mass production. In all too many instances though, little or no attention, it seems, is given to the contribution of hands. Repetitive work is allowed to merge in what comes through a modern factory. A pity, in many ways! At the least, a worker needs to see his or her effort in relation to the completed whole, assured of its worthwhileness, when it leaves the factory. This way, room may be found for what the new word calls "work satisfaction".

Without that, you and I may be excused for joining a modern poet, troubled about these things, who writes:

> I hate the whirr
>   Of machinery,
> Of wheels revolving
>   Ceaselessly.
>
> I mourn for man
>   Who once expressed
> Himself in work
>   With joyous zest.
>
> Who spent a craftsman's
>   Loving care,
> On wood or iron,
>   Or fabrics rare,
>
> But now must tend
>   These monsters grim
> Where factories make
>   A slave of him.
>
> Rod and piston,
>   Engine's heat;
> Belts rotating
>   Throb and beat.
>
> Machines, they haunt us
>   Everywhere;
> And now, alas,
>   Invade the air.

All slaves of speed,
  We live and die,
While peace and beauty
  Pass us by.

(Anon)

The relief from manual toil that many have long looked
forward to, has not turned out to be quite as idyllic as
expected. In the words of Dr J. S. Whale, the great
Christian interpreter of our times, "along with the internal
combustion engine there comes the slaughter on the roads;
along with aviation, bombs . . . The education which was
to have banished crime only makes crime more efficient,
increasing the range. Man's power to do good, is always
power to do more evil." Motors, one has to add, that can
take us from dull situations to fresh picnic spots and
beaches of good air and spacious views, can as easily take
us from the place of worship on Sundays. And with the
speed that motors afford, any day of our life, we can find
ourselves mingling with crowds, for whom we have no
individual care.

And there is no mechanical turning back – we have to
seek other solutions. Our Master knew nothing of factories
and speed, He travelled at no rate faster than He could
walk, or move on the back of a donkey. As part of the long-
time purpose of God, He was a craftsman, using His two
hands more effectively than many can today. And that, I
feel confident, made a good deal of difference as to how He
felt about a certain craftsman, who chanced to be at
worship, one Sabbath. (You will not be surprised that all
my life long, his has been one of my favourite stories,
preserved in the Gospels.) The man's plight, one feels
instinctively, was one to call out at once the compassion of
our Master. Three Gospel writers find room to record the
upset that day at worship (Matthew, Mark and Luke) but
only Dr Luke mentions that it was his *right* hand! (Luke
6:6–12; A.V.) That makes a great difference to how I

think of him. And to a one-time Craftsman and a doctor reporter, this would be enormously important. (A hand, in itself, as our modern-day dramatist, Christopher Fry, rejoices to remind us, is one of God's great gifts. "If one had never seen a hand," says Fry, "and were suddenly presented for the first time with this strange and wonderful thing, what a magnificently shocking and inexplicable and mysterious thing it would be!") But especially to a craftsman, surely! He may have had a family dependent on him – we don't know. Tradition, coming to us down the years, says he was a craftsman. In any case, a working man's daily wage at that time, was seldom, if ever, more than a silver coin worth nine old pence! With the best of management, sick pay, saved up for such an emergency, couldn't add up to a very handsome amount!

To the scribes and Pharisees, looking on, it was only an opportunity to judge the young Master Jesus, if He should dare to heal on the Sabbath. And He knew that! Luke says: "Looking round about them all, He said unto the man, 'Stretch forth thy hand!' And he did so; and *his hand was restored whole* as the other. And they were filled with madness; and communed one with another what they might do with Jesus."

"There is in this story", said my friend Dr William Barclay, "a glorious atmosphere of defiance. Jesus knew that He was being watched, but without hesitation, He healed. He bade the man stand out in the midst. The thing was not going to be done in a corner." True! There was great courage behind the happening – but I feel, even more, there was the fraternal understanding of a Craftsman, and also compassion. I am glad Dr Luke recorded it for us as he did – it is just the kind of story that would be close to his heart!

A writer in our day, using verse instead of prose, has tried to express something of the unforgettable outcome.

He makes the craftsman exclaim:

Hid in Our Hands

Praise God! Praise God! Give me my tools again!
Oh! Let me grasp a hammer and a saw!
Bring me a nail, and any piece of wood,
Come, see me shut my hand, and open it,
And watch my nimble fingers twirl a ring.
How good are solids! – oak and stone and iron,
And rough and smooth, and straight and curved and
   round!

I am a man again, a man for work,
A man for earning bread, and clothes and home;
A man, and not a useless hold-the-hand . . .
And ah . . . to think He goes about
So quietly, and does such things as this,
Making poor half-men whole!

(Anon)

Doodling, Here and There

Do you have a little pad beside your phone? I do, and so do many of my friends, as it's useful for jotting down names, addresses and dates. But also for more than that.

In the city on business this week, suddenly something cropped up that I needed to check. Being some miles from my flat, I was happy to remember that a good friend was no distance away, so I crossed the street to his office. He met me, as usual, with a smile. "No, it would be no bother at all", he assured me, and with that, he showed me into a little side office, where was a second phone. And the first thing I noticed, as I looked at the sturdy shelf on which the phone stood before me, was what I call "a doodling pad". I have never, till now, seen its name in print – indeed, I doubted whether it was a proper word. (But when I came back to my study, I looked it up, out of curiosity, in my monster *Britannica World Language Dictionary* – and there it was! True, it said that the word was colloquial, but immediately went on to say that its meaning was "*To draw pictures, symbols, etc, abstractedly, on whatever material comes to hand, while the mind is otherwise occupied*". This, of course, was what I had long understood by the word.)

But "doodling" is not an exercise occasioned solely by involved phonecalls. You may have noticed that. For some years, I was a member of a Board, meeting monthly, to deal with a costly matter of publishing. For a long while, I was the only woman, which I couldn't help feeling was a pity. For whatever little I was able to contribute, out of my experience, I learned a good deal there. I chanced to be seated often beside one of the really useful members of the Board; and each meeting, I noticed how much he "doodled". I realized early, that it wasn't that he was half-asleep, or unaware of what was going forward. Not at all! For after a good "doodle", he often arose to speak – it was just a little process that served his search for lucid thought.

And, it seems, there are many settings in which "doodling" can serve. I have for a long time now honoured Sir William Osler, the distinguished British doctor, lecturer and writer for doctors. He had a physique a lot smaller than the average, which might have been a factor contributing to his uncertainty, when the time came for him to decide what he wanted to do in life. A long time passed. He loved people – that was plain enough. More than that, he had been born to grow up loyal to his Christian upbringing in a Canadian home. But, amazing as it now seems, his great medical ministry nearly didn't happen. Osler got as far as Trinity College, as a young man, without being quite sure what he wanted to be. Then he happened upon a great encourager, James Bovell, M.D., M.R.C.P. He was a physiologist, and it was through him that the young man found his vocation, and was enabled to serve his God, and the world, so gloriously up until 1919. Lithe and quick, he held his first Chair of Medicine at McGill University; moving next to become Professor of Clinical Medicine at the University of Pennsylvania; on to the famous Johns Hopkins University; then on, after some time, to the Royal College of Physicians in London; and eventually to serve as Regius Professor of Medicine at Oxford. A versatile man, he is remembered to this hour with gratitude, by the many who profited from a teaching method he inaugurated, still known as "The Oslerian Method", whereby a young doctor was encouraged to concentrate on his patient, using his books and lectures merely as tools. Added to this, in time, his book *Principles and Practice of Medicine* became famous, appearing in many editions.

So it happened that whenever Osler found himself called to attend a long meeting of any sort, or to listen to a dull speech relating to the human world of suffering where he spent his gifts, it usually found him resorting to his own special kind of "doodling". He did not actually draw pictures or symbols abstractedly – he wrote on his pad his beloved encourager's name: "James Bovell, M.D., M.R.C.P."

*

And that's a nice thing to remember, looking back from this moment, as any one of us might do. *Encouragement is so important – to both giver and receiver!* And, fortunately, there are many ways in which it can be offered! It takes only a little lively imagination to find out the best way, under the circumstances!

One of the best ways, most of us discover, is to stand alongside some other person in need and to identify with any undertaking he or she is set upon. I saw the reality of this at a particular place in Dr Luke's "Acts of the Apostles". For the first fifteen chapters he reports what has happened to one another, in the hard, early days of the Christian Church. He says in effect, "they went here", "they went there", "they did this", "they did that"! Then suddenly, in what is now chapter 16 in our New Testament, there is a striking change. *He has now joined the company he is reporting on – and that must have been tremendously encouraging for them!* His reports come to us in what scholars call "the *we* passages"; he says, in effect, "*we* did this", "*we* suffered that", "*we* succeeded, here and there"! With that new emphasis, all is seen in a new light (Acts 16:10–17; 20:5–16; 21:1–18; 27:1–28; A.V.). It is to this day encouraging when a fellow believer, or fellow enthusiast, knowing what is going on, will leave his or her affairs, and come and help one!

Dr Leonard Small of Edinburgh has a delightful story about an old Scot, well up in his eighties, living in retirement in the city. In his time, he had been a famous Rugby forward for Oxford University and Scotland. "Still, to this day," says Dr Small, "he and another member of the same Oxford team gather on the day of the Universities match, put on their Oxford caps, and sit there in their dressing-gowns and bedroom slippers round the television set, hardly able to sit still, *wanting Oxford to win*!" Great encouragers!

And, thank God, there have always been those in our midst! Life here could only poorly stagger on without them! In the early days of the Christian witness, Paul, often hard pressed, wrote to his friends in Rome: "I want to be among you to be myself encouraged by your faith, as well as you by mine" (Romans 1:12; N.E.B.).

Sometimes it's not possible to be physically present with those on whom we depend for encouragement. Paul found that, again and again, even as we do. He kept on journeying; but he kept on writing letters, too. After he had left Thessalonica, for instance, he wrote to thank them for news, and to tell them what an encouragement they were; Dr J. B. Phillips, in our day, put his message into modern speech: "To know that you are standing fast in the Lord, is indeed a breath of life to us" (1 Thessalonians 3:8). Thessalonica was a great city, of some two hundred thousand people (still, under the name of Salonika, it holds seventy thousand). In Paul's day it was a free city – that is, it had never suffered the indignity of having Roman troops quartered within it, though its main street was part of the very road which linked Rome with the East. It was, therefore, an important city in those early days of missionary strategy. And a great deal depended on those within, and those, like Paul, who came and went, keeping up their courageous Christian witness. They had to support each other, through prayer, and letter writing. To this end, Paul set himself to write, in what is now the Second Letter to his fellow Christians in Thessalonica: "May the Lord Jesus Christ and God our Father (Who has loved us *and given us unending encouragement* and unfailing hope by His grace) inspire you with courage and confidence in every good thing you say or do" (Dr J. B. Phillips's translation,

Letters to Young Churches).

What an encouraging prayer; set in a letter!

Some ministers, deaconesses and youth leaders known to me, still in these modern times make good use of letters. Though they are never collected, as in Dr Luke's and Paul's day, nor shared as widely. But they are not tossed into the waste paper basket either – they are too precious for that. "I do not think it is realized", wrote one who discovered their worth in our day, "how much help and encouragement can sometimes be sent through the postman. If you look into your own memory," he goes on, "you will probably find that the encouragement, or the comfort, that some letters once brought is amongst your most cherished possessions. A letter to someone going through rough times, or far away, or starting a new work, or a birthday or an anniversary remembered, are amongst those signs of human interest and affection which I think should come from the love of God – no one is too busy to think out acts like this, so simple and yet so grateful to those who receive them."

Perhaps you have a loved encourager of your own, whose name you "doodle" on an agenda paper during meetings!

Mothers Manage It

Moving up from Elizabeth and Mary to our own day, it is plain to the least observant amongst us, that mothers are of many kinds. Most are loved within the family and respected beyond it – but there are unhappy exceptions.

For several years I served in a Social Service Mission in our largest city, during a country-wide economic depression, and there I had to do with both mothers and children. It was a hard time for most, but the magnificent spirit of many of those mothers with whom I had to do daily, filled me with admiration.

To our Sunday School came one afternoon a small boy, new to me. He said his name was "Davy". He was well-patched – but well-scrubbed, and well-mannered. "I would like to send a message to your mother, Davy", I said, as he was about to leave. "Will you tell her that I will pop in on Wednesday afternoon. I hope I'll know her. Is she pretty?"

"I don't know", was his ten-year-old boy's answer. "But she's a pretty good cook. And she's pretty fair, when kids get in a fight."

*

Elizabeth's or Mary's sons might have given a different answer, either at ten or as teenagers. I wonder?

Helen Sushames, a modern Christian mother with teenagers, had something to say on this issue, within my hearing the other day. And when I told her I was writing on how "mothers manage", she kindly gave me her permission to quote her. I liked the way she began – just where she was: "I live with several teenagers. I haven't much choice, really, seeing I'm their mother."

A lot of what she told me, didn't surprise me. I'm not a mother; but I lived once for several years in somebody else's home, where there were several lively teenagers, and I learned a lot from them. (But I mustn't break in on Helen's experience.)

"Now and then," she went on, "I wondered why no one ever warned me that 'dear little babies' grow up into *teenagers*. Sometimes, I'm positive that my teenagers run my home – overrun might be more accurate. We tune in to *their* kind of radio station. The TV often seems to be *so* loud! They can't stand my favourites . . . And one of my sons", she added, "plays the cornet." (I know what that means: I once had as neighbour a youth who, the minute he came indoors, played his, and near my study, his old-fashioned upstairs window open all the summer!) "And my daughter", she added, immediately I was ready to go on lending a listening ear, "strums her guitar – and usually when the TV and radio are on.

"What's more", Helen went on, drawing a second breath, "they're always hungry, and 'fixing themselves a feed', as they call it. After that, there's the problem of who's going to clean up . . .

"I listen to their opinions . . .

"One minute, the house is seething with my teenagers and their friends – the next minute, I'm alone in a deserted battle-field . . .

"But wait . . . Am I beginning to get this all out of perspective?" she queried. "What about when these same children show remarkable insight and sensitivity? This happens quite often, really. What about their strong sense of justice; and their loyal love for me, and each other? And what about our family traditions, and jokes, to say nothing of the crises and problems – the sharing of things – which draw us closer together? Isn't this what makes up family life?"

I like to credit myself with being an interested listener

to this kind of talk – anyway, Helen went on: "Life with my teenagers is exciting and unpredictable . . . Was I like this when I was a teenager? Was I? *Full* of contrasts like these children of mine? They're so *full of energy – yet so tired! Intolerant – yet so loving! Confident – yet so fearful!*"

Then on she went after a pause, to share a prayer she had fashioned as a mother: "Lord, help me to understand, and cope. Help me to guide them to mature adulthood. Let me trust them to be themselves. Lord, I wonder what You were like, when You were a teenager? Did Your mother, Mary, always understand You? Somehow, I don't think she did. Especially, when You stayed in the Temple – without reference to Your parents – on that trip to Jerusalem. You certainly caused consternation . . . But now I'm glad scripture records that story." And so are many others of us. We owe a debt to Dr Luke for the way he set it down: "*Jesus grew . . . in body, and in wisdom, gaining favour with God, and men*" (Luke 2:52; Good News Bible).

Every year the parents of Jesus went to Jerusalem for the Passover Festival. When Jesus was twelve years old they went to the Festival as usual. When the Festival was over, they started back home, but the boy Jesus stayed in Jerusalem. His parents did not know this; they thought that He was with the group, so they travelled a whole day and started looking for Him among their relatives and friends. They did not find Him, so they went back to Jerusalem looking for Him. On the third day, they found Him in the Temple, sitting with the Jewish teachers, listening to them and asking questions. All who heard Him were amazed at His intelligent answers.

"His parents were astonished when they saw Him, and His mother said to Him, 'My son, why have You done this to us? Your father and I have been terribly worried trying to find You.'

"He answered them, 'Why did you have to look for me?

63

Didn't you know that I had to be in my Father's house?'
But they did not understand His answer.

"So Jesus went back with them to Nazareth, where He
was obedient to them. *His mother treasured all these things
in her heart.*"

A beautiful sentence, that! Is there a good mother of a
budding teenager anywhere who finds no need to do the
same? I doubt it. At any rate, I find Helen Sushames
identifying herself with the experience of the long-ago
village mother, of whom it was first spoken.

And in her prayer as a modern mother, she says: "It
makes You seem so much more real . . . But it also says
– to gladden my motherly heart – that You grew . . . And
You came home," she continues, "and were subject to
Your parents (Luke 2:51).

"But, life wasn't quite the same in Your day, was it,
Lord? You must have had early responsibilities in that
carpenter's shop. Especially . . . as time passed and You
were the oldest son of a widowed mother. And I often
wonder how she coped with it all.

"I think it's all a matter of loving and respecting each
other, as people. And my teenagers *are* people," she adds,
"just as I am a person.

"I am glad You understand, Lord, and remain present
with me.

"Thank You for my maddening, challenging teenagers!"

*

It would be nice to have today some of Mary's mothering
prayers, but these are not given us – each mother,
entrusted by God with such a task, must make her own. A
woman poet of our day, in a tender poem, suggests that
there was need of divine support from the start, in that
special task Mary had been given as a mother. It begins:

> When Jesus was a little thing,
> His mother, in her hood of blue,

Called to Him, through the dusk of Spring:
   "Jesus, my Jesus, where are you?"

Caught in a gust of whirling bloom,
   She stood a moment at the door,
Then lit the candle in the room,
   In its pink earthen bowl of yore.

The little Jesus saw it all –
   The blur of yellow in the street;
The fair trees by the tumbling wall;
   The shadowy other lads, whose feet

Struck a quick noise from out the grass;
   He saw, dim in the halflit air;
As one sees folk within a glass,
   His mother with her candle there.
     "Jesus! Jesus!"

                    (Anon)

She writes on the assumption that when the twelve-year-old got lost during the trip to Jerusalem, for the Feast of the Passover, it wasn't the first time. We have no records from Dr Luke or anybody else concerning this – nothing, save the discovery of good mothers everywhere, that such happenings are not solitary. (If there is any factual truth behind this little poem, then Mary kept *that* too in the secret places of her mother-heart. It could have happened. For He was, from the start, a very natural boy – we can be sure of that!)

                   *

Some years ago, an American woman, Anna Jarvis, encouraged her own and many churches round the world, to mark off an agreed day on the calendar as "Mothers' Day". The idea spread, and its promoter was credited with having enriched the world with a worthy idea. But, here and there, speakers grew weakly sentimental, until what came forth was no tribute to the mothers many of us knew: sensible, gentle, strong, practical, and fun-loving!

Then, encouraging the presentation of Mothers' Day gifts, the opportunity was blatantly commercialized, to the diminishing of those essential qualities of spirit shown us in Mary, the mother of our Lord! So Mothers' Day, as a festival of thanks, was replaced in many worshipping congregations by Family Day. This way, it is more difficult to be sentimental; and easier to see mother in her God-given setting!

When first I began to ponder the wonder of this plan of creation, preservation and direction, I spoke of a secret desire I had to write an anthem. My family at once asked me what verse of scripture I meant to use. And I had to confess that the words I had set my heart on were not in most Bibles – though I hastened to add that I had copied them into mine: "A Woman's Work is Never Done!" Great words! If ever a text was worthy to go into the Bible, surely this is!

I have heard many a woman here and there misuse it, when her washing won't dry, or there seems no end to her cooking: "Ah, a woman's work is never done!" But that is to be blind to the whole point I am making. The words in no sense spell out exasperation; but rather the exultation of wonder! *A truly ongoing gift of rich life, unending!*

So I would have my sopranos sing: "A woman's work is never done!" And then the contraltos would come in with: "Never done, never done, never done!" And I would have the tenors strengthen the reality of it with "Never done, never done!" And in turn the basses would rumble down below: "Never done, never done!" And we'd all sing it, and sing it until the real wonder and beauty of it entered our souls anew, and every woman of us stood up a little straighter, to serve more joyously. And this way, it would *go on through the generations*! For this is the way God has planned it! *Strong and beautiful, in many places! Fragile in some! But God hasn't thought out any better way to do it!*

Bumping the Stars

Another birthday!

And the further I go along this human way, the more heartily I find myself agreeing with Walter de la Mare: "Merely to be alive is adventure enough in a world like this, so erratic and disjoined; so lovely and so odd, and mysterious and profound. It is, at any rate, a pity to remain in it half-dead!"

And the people one meets! Especially in growing up – how important! Lowell never forgot the effect Emerson had on him when he was part of a young group of students. They came in, and went out, but never the same! "We went out", said Lowell, years later, "not knowing exactly what he had said, *but with our heads bumping the stars!*"

That's it! He was speaking poetically, of course, but something had happened – and very real it was! I've been a student to such a master, as had Daniel George, eager to say: "Youth is a splendid time. Everybody ought to be young once!"

So I feel, and it ought to be part of one's spiritual growth. It's a tragedy to travel through life's days and nights "half-dead", to borrow de la Mare's words. I have no need to turn up my own words (that in maturity, I found pleasure in setting down in an early page of my autobiography) but here they are, for all that. For without the spirituality they spelled out for me, there is no understanding all that life has brought me, to this hour! I was in my teens, still at home in the village. The little Wesleyan Chapel stood on the opposite corner. I was seldom absent at service time, but shy, as many, I have since discovered, are at that age. I was going through a stage of spiritual "growing pains".

(Who among us can guess what baffles a teenager? There are words to describe outward things, even one's sensations of joy and pain, but none, it seems, for the secret traffickings of one's spirit.)

A visiting missioner put in an appearance, and people gathered from near and far to hear him at the village hall. There was nothing especially emotional – and just as well. For all along, I had stoutly refused to be "stormed" into the Kingdom. I waited for a moment when my mind would give assent to my emotions. And something told me it was only a matter of time, before I must decide as surely as anything in my life till then – and till now – Whose I was, and Whom I meant to serve. A profound experience! Explain it? I could not then, and I cannot fully now, any more than I might explain the coming of the dawn. It was a miracle that touched my life. It is too much, even to this day, to ask for words adequately to hold down such an experience – the whole of life, as it opens out, is left for that!

> The earth and every common sight
> To me did seem
> Apparelled in celestial light:
> The glory and the freshness of a dream!

Still, as days passed, I knew I had no words yet to lace it to reality! And as I speak of it now, after so many rewarding years, it pleases me to lay hold of Lowell's lovely expression. The old evangelical term "Conversion" had been long spoiled for me, by some who used it too glibly, too piously, robbing it of its essential living glory.

In due time, I came upon Masefield's "Everlasting Mercy", with its glad story of Saul Kane; in his own way, he also was "bumping his head on the stars", as surely as I was myself. At the word of a Quaker girl, he felt within him that, to use his own words, "Christ had given him birth". Nothing in the world about him, from that hour, felt the same, or looked the same. He found himself singing:

O glory of the lighted mind
How dead I'd been, how dumb, how blind.
The station brook, to my new eyes,
Was bubbling out of Paradise,
The waters rushing from the rain
Were singing, "Christ is risen again!"
I thought all earthly creatures knelt
From rapture of the joy I felt.
The narrow station wall's brick ledge,
The wild hop withering in the hedge,
The lights in Huntsman's upper storey
Were parts of an eternal glory!

And so it surely was to young Peter and Andrew and companions, beside the lake waters of Galilee! They lived there, handy-by; they knew the toil it took to keep boats trim, and to catch fish; they knew the joys of companionship, and the vagaries of the market. But all was changed for them when Jesus came that way and called for their allegiance. Life wasn't a little local thing any more. It had burst out into a new dimension. In time, it would encompass the world! And it all started there beside the lake – with its so commonplace trappings!

They were surprisingly young! I used to think otherwise, misled by the pictures in Bibles and books. All the men whom I knew were then clean-shaven, in their young years – only men older than my father, and as old as my grandfather, wore beards. Today, it is easy to appreciate the fact that the disciples whom the Young Master called, were also young, energetic men, now that there are so many bearded men amongst us.

As time went by, Dr Luke recorded the scene, in what is now chapter 5 of his Gospel, that has come down the centuries. Jesus was again on the familiar lake shore, and there He saw "two ships standing; but the fishermen were gone out of them, and were washing their nets". (I find it easy enough to visualize them; as I read those words, I see busy young men, bronzed by the sun and air, as fit as He Who called them.) "And He entered into one of the ships which was Simon's," says Dr Luke, "and prayed him that he would thrust out a little from the land. And He sat down, and taught the people out of the ship." (And it's easy from that time on, at least, to see that the young men involved were not total strangers. They'd had this chance, if no other, of considering the challenge of the Young Master's teaching, before joining up with the Twelve. And a challenge it was – enough to stir *young* men!)

Time passed, and the faithful scribe continued with his record, as we have it now in Luke's Gospel, chapter 6, verse 13, reading, "And when it was day, He called unto Him His disciples: and of them He chose twelve, whom also he named apostles: Simon (whom He also named Peter), and Andrew his brother, James and John, Philip and Bartholomew, Matthew and Thomas, James the son of Alphaeus, and Simon called Zelotes, and Judas the brother of James, and Judas Iscariot, which also was the traitor."

And much more happened that only found a place in secular records. Pliny, Roman writer of the first century (A.D. 23 to 79), was soon busy informing the emperor that the thing most remarkable about the "new sect" was that the members of it kept singing when they met, as others did not – kept singing hymns to Christ Jesus! The truth was, in the most spiritual sense, that these were men and women who, by Him, had been enabled to "bump their heads on the stars"! They moved in a new dimension. They couldn't help it; they were joyous, and they sang!

Clement of Alexandria was busy in the second century, reporting much the same – and it was good news in a grey world of carelessness and cruelty, opening out to Christianity! His observation was concerned not only with new values observed in the place of worship, *but also in the*

71

place of work. "Holding festival, then," wrote he, "in our whole life, we cultivate our fields, praising; we sail the seas, hymning; in all the rest of our conversation we conduct ourselves according to rule." But it was an exalted Christian rule!

Centuries on, Jerome had much the same story to tell: "The ploughman at his plough", he found joy in reporting, "sings his hallelujahs; the busy mower refreshes himself with psalms; the vine-dresser sings the songs of David."

"All", wrote Chrysostom, still later, "come together with us to sing, and in it they unitedly join; the young and the old, the rich and the poor, women and men, slaves and free!"

When we come to Dr James Denny, great Scottish interpreter of things Christian, we are only a step away from our own generation. When he left his pulpit in the church in Broughty Ferry, for a Professor's Chair in Glasgow, many a student, in a new way, found himself "bumping his head on the stars". He brought to the religious experience of many a one, a new dimension. Someone said of the Principal, a lovely thing: "It was by his deeply reverent, yet calm, confident handling of the mysteries of the Faith that he 'sent his hearers forth with uplifted head, taking to their souls the things for ever sure, though the heavens should fall'."

We live, in many ways, in a different world today – but the world in which we live needs nothing so much as men and women who, challenged by Christ, find themselves living in a glorious dimension, "bumping their heads on the stars".

All to His Glory

I don't know how long I'd been asleep – we had joined the plane very early – but suddenly I was awake, and the dawn was coming in through my window. Next moment, an official appeared in the aisle, and steadying his pace as he approached my seat, I asked him: "What mountain is that I see?"

Without any hesitancy, he answered me, "Hermon!"

And that properly wakened me. For we were to stop down in the little land where our Lord and Master was born, grew up, and ministered. In a short while we would be there. In the meantime, my thoughts were all of those men whom He took with Him up that highest mountain in Syria, and there, where one of the greatest events of their lives took place, they'd fallen asleep, as soundly as I had. I had always thought of Hermon as "The Mount of Transfiguration", its name meaning "sanctuary" or "apart", which seemed so suitable, although there was no actual mention of its name in either Mark's Gospel, or in Luke 9:28–42 (A.V.). The Eastern Church, to this day, holds that this memorable happening took place on the top of Mount Tabor, not Mount Hermon. And though they still call their Festival of the Transfiguration "The Taborion", this seems strange. For a long time now, our scholars have pointed this out. "It may be", wrote Dr William Barclay, "that the choice of Tabor is based on the mention of Mount Tabor, in Psalm 89:12; but it is an unfortunate choice. Tabor is in the south of Galilee, and Caesarea Philippi is away to the north. Tabor is no more than a thousand feet high, and, in the time of Jesus, there was a fortress on the top. It is much more likely that this happened amidst the eternal snows of Mount Hermon,

73

which is 9,200 feet high, much nearer Caesarea Philippi, and where the solitude would be much more complete." There was, I'd always noticed, some slight variance in the reports – but who would have expected otherwise? It was an altogether amazing event to report at all!

The mountain has three peaks, with that on the south-east the highest. Snow lay on the summit most of the year, and for a good deal of the rest of the time, was found in the ravines.

The four men – Jesus and His close friends – must have climbed steadily up that chosen mountain I'd looked down upon, perhaps even silently, until they reached remote solitude. High above the common world's affairs, the air must have seemed pure and tonic, the silence absolute. It was a wholly fit place for contemplation and prayer. If anywhere, there the spirit might pierce the material, and become absorbed with the Unseen.

But there the disciples *fell asleep*. Poor men! Frail human beings, like the rest of us! It is an example of the honesty of the New Testament that their lapse is recorded; but it was even more a matter for praise that they didn't stay asleep. For the record says this unforgettable thing, and to me it is precious: "*When they were awake they saw His glory.*" (That comes out of Luke's account of the total happening. I like that!)

But what does it mean? Before we come to the word translated by "glory", there's the word "sleep". That has an earthly sound about it, so that when we are trying to understand it, we are beginning very close to our own experience. Even riding high over the land, flying to Palestine, one can't keep awake all the time, sleep so naturally lays its hold.

We can, of course, consider it in its most literal sense, as well as in its deeper spiritual sense. To be "asleep", as the Oxford Dictionary defines it, "with eyes closed, muscles relaxed, nervous system inactive, consciousness nearly suspended", is one thing; but to be asleep in mind and spirit is something more, and over and over in the New Testament the word "sleep" is used in this significant sense. "It is high time to wake out of sleep"; "Awake to righteousness and sin not"; and again: "Awake, thou that sleepest, and arise from the dead, and Christ shall give thee light." It is in this sense that Dr Halford Luccock used the term in speaking to the students of Yale Divinity School: "I feel", he said, "that a case could be made out for the statement that the deadliest enemy of preaching today is not atheism or communism, but sleep."

What exactly did Peter, James and John see? But who can analyse Glory? We lose in explanation what can only be caught in experience. "They saw His glory" – and it was a glory that outshone the very greatest of their leaders, Moses; and the very greatest of their preachers, Elijah. More than that we cannot say. We can only say what we see "when we wake" – and that is not easily said, either. Irenaeus, one of the early Church fathers, declared tellingly: "The Glory of God is man fully alive!" (That would certainly apply to Christ!) "The very word *glory*", to use Dr William Barclay's comment, "is a more than human word. We use the word loosely of the kind of honour and reputation and fame that some kind of human achievement can bring; but properly, *glory* belongs to God alone." In the library at Buckingham Palace is a magnificent collection of musical scores by Handel, each autographed and bearing the letters S.D.G., standing for *Soli Deo Gloria*, which is, "Glory to God alone"!

Near the city of Rio de Janeiro is a Children's Home, which bears the name of *Instituto Ana Gonzaga*, linking the joyous miracle of its compassion with the woman who built it and opened wide its doors. When one day the committee suggested she should have her portrait painted and hung in the Home, her reply was instant: "Don't you dare . . . ! *The Home is not for my glory, but for the Glory of God!*"

We see this Glory in the face of Jesus – that is the meaning of His Incarnation. First of all, there is the Glory

75

of His humanity. Some, up through the years, have tried to solve certain perplexities they have, by denying this in its fullness. Some have contended that it was but an appearance, a phantom; but the New Testament, from beginning to end, is a protest against such a view. "The Word became Flesh," wrote John, "*and we beheld His Glory, the Glory as of the only Begotten of the Father, full of grace and truth.*" He was no pale-faced young man, beautifully other-worldly, with a flabby forearm, and a glad-to-die expression. Far from it. He was truly human. He spent a good deal of His time out of doors. His mind grew, as well as His body – a reality that some find it difficult to take in. But accept it, we must. He had to learn all manner of ordinary boyish, young-manly, human things; Luke says: "Jesus grew both in body and in wisdom, gaining favour with God and men" (Luke 2:52; G.N.B.). His very humanity precluded an overall omniscience, as we understand it; even when an adult, He had sometimes to ask questions such as "Who touched My garments?" of some who jostled Him in a crowd, wherein a needy woman sought healing. And again, of the father of an epileptic boy at the bottom of that very mountain where He had been transfigured – for He could not stay there, all too soon He had to move amidst needy humanity – "How long", He asked the distressed father, "is it since this came upon him?"

Jesus loved, He grieved, He showed indignation, He was tempted; He delighted in the innocent company of little children, and all manner of men. He mingled with those with whom He shared life – in its joy, and in its sorrow. Right at the very beginning of His public ministry, He accepted an invitation to a wedding. And we do not forget the occasion when under His country's scorching midday sun, He had to take a rest at a well-side, and ask a woman for a drink of cold water. At another time, He clearly showed His understanding of what a poet of our day calls "the strong crust of friendly bread". He fed five thousand on that occasion, and four thousand on another; and brought forth bread, to carry a symbolic meaning for ever amongst His followers, at His Last Supper with them. That was the most precious thing He had to give them as a parting gift – He had no valuable possessions; and the day came when the soldiers took even His seamless robe.

I shall always be grateful for that splendid little book from my Yorkshire friend, Dr W. R. Maltby, beloved Warden of Ilkley Deaconess College, *The Significance of Jesus*. "If we claim", he wrote, "that some significance of Jesus has been recovered for our day, that presumes that something has been lost. To put the gains in a word," he went on, "we have recovered the truth of the real humanity of our Lord. It is difficult to realize how largely that truth had been lost, even while it stood in the recited creeds, and called to men from the pages of the Book they revered . . ."

The Glory of His divinity, it had to be realized, had to be coupled with His humanity, not only when He stepped out from the carpenter's workshop and set out to teach and preach and heal, but all the way through. Without that balance, He couldn't have sustained His heavy itineraries, much less the claims He made for Himself: His oneness with God. Had He looked like many of the mediaeval artists made Him to appear, that claim would have been one of either blasphemy or human madness. For it was a great claim. It can only be because we have grown used to it that we have easily settled to it. Even more persuasive is the fact that His disciples – close to Him day by day, in freshness and in natural weariness, in private and in public, in life and death (and such a death!) – utterly believed His claim; and that, against all their upbringing. "Hear, O Israel, the Lord our God *is one God*", was the call with which every synagogue service began. Yet they believed their Master when He claimed oneness with God; believed Him utterly – not only that close little company of disciples, but others who also followed: men, women, and children, Mary with her acclaim "Master!" and Thomas, with his problem of doubt shed by the sight of the nail-prints, moving him to a triumphant cry: "My Lord, and my God!"

This is the Glory that I see – *the Glory of His humanity, the Glory of His divinity* – now that, with countless others, I have "come awake". It is my joy to sing with others in the congregation:

> In the name of Jesus
> Every knee shall bow,
> Every tongue confess Him
> *King of Glory now*;
> 'Tis the Father's pleasure
> We should call Him Lord,
> Who from the beginning
> Was the mighty Word!

The Endless Furrow

A good deal of my working life has been spent in the world's great cities, and I owe them a debt for historical reminders of human struggle, riches of art and music and literature, and architectural beauty. But I am at heart a country lover; by that, I mean, I love the country in all her moods, and in all her labours; and this isn't only a matter of full sunshine, and spring hopefulness, though there is nothing lovelier. I wish I knew the name of "Dear Anonymous" who shared with me, one spring in the English Cotswolds, the following poem:

> The waiting fields
>   are ready now
> For steady hands
>   *upon the plough*,
> For quickening seed,
>   and gentle rain,
> For body's toil
>   and sweat and pain,
> And sturdy faith
>   that sees ahead
> In bare brown earth
>   tomorrow's bread.

It might have come from a sturdy ploughman whom I saw one morning in the Cotswolds, coming up over a gentle slope, with his plough and two white horses. We met, and spent a few memorable moments together, at the end of the furrow. His name, I learned, was Mr Lapford, and the names of his two beautiful horses, which he allowed me to photograph, "Prince" and "Darling". (And that close-up

is one of the most treasured to come from my old camera.
I inserted it later as an illustration of my book *Seven Days
of the Week*.)

I was able to tell him that I had been born on a farm, and
had many a time, season by season, followed my father in
the furrow. "I been at it", said Mr Lapford, "since I was
thirteen. Tractors have the speed, but it's horses does the
job. Of course, there's lots of walking," he had to add, "but
I don't know about these sittin' jobs. There's more
companionship with horses." And when I had taken my
treasured photograph – which I promised to send to him
later, and did – he was happy to add: "Yes, they know me
when I call 'em early in the morning."

*

Of course, a lot depends on the character of the
ploughman. Such a one, close to Mr Lapford's heart, lies
no great distance from where I was born and grew up. In
rural Waimea West, half a world away from where he was
born. His stone reads:

> John Kerr, arrived 1841, born Midlothian. First man to
> thrust a plough into the soil of the province, by his
> industry, intelligence and upright character he earned
> for himself a handsome competence and the esteem of
> his fellow-colonists.

There will be no one now in Waimea West who remembers
him; but his achievement is a wonderful inspiration.

Our Lord spoke about the ploughman, and His striking
words have come down to us thanks to Dr Luke, who set
them for us in his Gospel: "*No man, having put his hand
to the plough, and looking back, is fit for the Kingdom of
God*" (9:62; A.V.). Jesus doubtless had dealings with
many ploughmen, in the village carpenter's workshop.
There were always beams to be made, and to be mended.
The primitive wooden plough common in New Testament

times was simpler than any today; but the essentials of which Jesus spoke, in teaching His listeners the Christian Way of Life, have never changed.

The only way to plough a *straight furrow* – as I early learned in the countryside – is to keep one's eyes steadily on some set mark at the far end of the field. If one ever looked back, to see with pride how very straight his furrow was, and how far he'd come, his plough would be likely to swerve. As one has said: "*The hand guides the plough – but the eye guides the hand.*" (Ask yourself, sometime, a very deep Christian question: "Is my furrow straight?")

Interpreting our Lord's words, Dr Barclay found occasion to underline this. He saw, he confessed, so many of us looking back. "There are some", he said, "whose hearts are in the past. Such walk for ever looking backwards, and thinking wistfully of the good old days." (Natural enough, for some of us, as years add up – but dangerous!)

*

But there is forgiveness – even for a defaulting ploughman. That is part of the message of Mercy that our Lord brought to us! I find it pleasantly put for me, in a simple word picture I've treasured through the years, which tells of a young ploughman, with gentle encouragement. "The hand that guided the plough", it says, "had not weathered many seasons, and often the furrows were crooked . . . The ploughman finished, and looked sorrowfully at the field; he was disheartened and pained by the crooked furrows that glared like great scars on the landscape. The weeks passed and the young blades of corn formed a carpet of green lines, only revealing more clearly the crookedness of the furrows. The months passed . . . until harvest showed a golden sea of waving stems unbroken and unmarred. The young ploughman gazed once more upon his field, and his face shone . . . 'There's many a full sack', said he, 'comes from a crooked furrow!'"

*

It's wonderful both to start – *and to start again*! That, whatever the years have brought of good harvest, or poor harvest, is "the glory of going on"! This faced me strikingly after two successive Services of Holy Communion I shared. At both, the celebrant read the ancient words: "Ye therefore that do truly and earnestly repent of your sins, and are in love and charity with your neighbours, *and intend to lead a new life*, draw near with faith, and take this holy sacrament to your comfort, and make your humble confession to Almighty God."

The first of these two Services found me kneeling beside a young girl I knew, at this very beginning of her Christian life, her "endless furrow". She was now someone with every right to be present in that service of Faith, for she did "intend to lead a new life"! She rose expectantly, at the beginning of the furrow! I shall never forget that shared experience!

And the next Service of Communion I was privileged to attend was no less memorable. The same gracious words were spoken by the same celebrant. Beside me, this time, knelt an old business friend, an alcoholic until lately. And as we heard those words, I knew that he did "intend to lead a new life"! He was beginning again! Hands to the plough, feet in the furrow, eyes ahead, lifted high with a God-given sense of direction, and hopefulness!

My simple prayer for each of them, as those two Services ended, was one that I've prayed many a time myself:

Keep me from turning back!
My hand is on the plough, my faltering hand:
But all in front of me is untilled land.
Keep me from turning back,
The shares with rust are spoiled – and yet – and yet –
My Lord! My Lord! Keep me from turning back!

(Anon)

But Two Words

I've often been out fishing and caught nothing. Have you?

Early in Luke's Gospel comes that unforgettable story of Peter the fisherman and his friends, and it has remained a favourite with me (Luke 5:1–7; A.V.). They were none of them amateurs, but had fished for their living all their lives. I thought of them – and that challenge to "*Try again!*" that made all the difference – when I visited the Sea of Galilee, where it happened.

Peter, I can understand, was in a low mood when the Master spoke to him – piqued, if you like – when He said: "Let down your nets for a draught!" His retort was: "We have toiled all the night, and taken nothing!"

But it didn't end there! "Nevertheless", Peter found the courage to reply when he heard that challenging "*Try again!*", "at Thy word I will let down the net." And the Gospel records, "when they had this done, they enclosed a great multitude of fishes" (v. 6). And it seems to me, on reflection, that life is often like that.

We are not all fishermen, we find our daily work in all sorts of settings; and we're not all saints, as Peter later became. But in this record of an experience that turned from failure to success, there is something for us all. The truth is, we can't get along without lending an ear to that seemingly simple command: "*Try again!*"

Someone has said: "The perseverance of the saints consists in ever new beginnings!"

It was certainly so with Peter.

And it was so with John Wesley!

There was no forgetting his Aldersgate experience, and it stood meaningfully in the life of many another who followed the same Lord. Years later Wesley said, realistically: "Our societies were formed from those who were wandering upon the dark mountains – that belonged to no Christian Church; but were awakened by the preaching of the Methodists, who had pursued them through the wilderness of this world to the highways and the hedges, to the markets and the fairs, to the hills and the dales – who set up the standard of the Cross in the streets and lanes of the cities, in the villages, in the barns, and farmers' kitchens, etc. – *and all this done in such a way, and to such an extent, as never had been done before since the Apostolic age.*"

And the challenge goes on, into our own day. Dr John Baillie reminds us of it, and very strikingly, when he says: "To those who know a little of Christian history, probably the most moving of all the reflections it brings is *not* the thought of the great events and the well-remembered saints, but of those innumerable millions of entirely obscure faithful men and women, every one with his or her own individual hopes and fears and joys and sorrows and loves – and sins and temptations and prayers – once every whit as vivid and alive as mine are now . . . Each of them worshipped at the Eucharist and found their thoughts wandering *and tried again.*"

We belong to that company, we are people who have quite unexpectedly at times found our concentration at prayer lapsing. Or our churchgoing – we don't seem to be getting anything out of it. Or we don't any longer, we find, take the pride we once felt in giving to good causes.

What has happened? In our own setting, it can be that we've "toiled all the night, and taken nothing". We need to hear, as did John Baillie, before he was in a position to set down those striking words for us in *A Reasoned Faith* (Oxford University Press), the equivalent of "*Try again!*" And wanting strength and a readiness to respond, and perhaps even the inclination to do so, we need to lay hold of the presence and power of Christ to change things. Our future depends on it!

Kagawa, the disowned, knew this in our day; and so did Hugh Redwood, the journalist, lacking a Christian experience; and Lilian Cox, the eager teacher, already a Christian, writing tellingly:

> Ready I stand for any new adventure.
> What dost Thou say? "The sea still waits My will;
> Launch the old boat again, and be a fisher still."

This is one of the most challenging things about a relationship with our Lord and Master. It comes alive for me every time I go to Holy Communion, and hear the words of the Service addressed to me, as one among those who "intend to lead a new life".

It can't be done alone – but it can be done!

That became gloriously real to me, when as a guest of my dear Bill and Ethel Topliss, in Derbyshire, we motored across country and came to the Chapel of Kelham College, Nottinghamshire. They had never been there and neither had I. There we looked on a masterpiece of sculpture, the work of a young craftsman, Charles Jagger. It's a figure of the Christ, bound to His Cross, and the effect is one of great power, His eyes looking straight into the eyes of whoever looks up at Him.

When first the young sculptor, setting out to portray his Lord, sought to show His gentleness, it looked like weakness; and when he struggled to show His strength, it looked like hardness. And Jagger knew the bitterness of failure. But as he cast himself down in that moment, it seemed to him that into his studio came the Christ, Risen and Triumphant, saying with the compassion Peter knew, the two words: "*Try again!*" And the instant that the failure and the Living Christ were face to face, things were different – and that difference stands now in Kelham College, for all to see.

There is no Christian promise, of course, that, in the undertakings that are ours in this life, we will be saved from "empty boats"; but there is the promise that when that comes, we shall find ourselves in the presence of One Who is forgiving and supporting, and saying with all-seeing eyes looking into a new future: "*Try again!*" The secret of the adequacy of fisherman Peter, and of Jagger, and of many another of us, lies here. It is not just stopping to call up reserves and screw up courage – how many times we have done that! After a Communion Service we have told ourselves we will try harder. We have stood out alone under the great stars, and not once but many times, a sense of failure has risen up and blurred them; many another of us has taken into enfolding arms a new little life – so small, so utterly dependent – and we have said, one by one, unknown to any other: "I'll be a better man now!", "I'll be a better woman!" But as we look at Peter, at Charles Jagger, and at ourselves, we see that just trying harder is not a gospel at all: the real Gospel is in our laying down our human failure at the feet of the Risen Christ, and appropriating His forgiveness and His enduring power. It is in letting Him grip our lives with His new purpose; it is in living in His unfailing presence; it is in surrendering to the very Highest all our faltering gifts of personality, knowing, feeling, willing. This turns failure inside out, and makes it one of life's amazements – and why should it not be so? Did He not say: "*Lo, I am with you always, even unto the end of the world . . . all power is given unto Me*"?

Faith means counting on Him

> Whose presence is not bound
> To vast cathedrals, and the light that falls
> Through many-tinted glass. His voice and touch are found
> Within the poorest doors, the humblest walls.
>
> He sits at table with the tired and poor,
> He shares the fire-place with the spent and old,
> He keeps with suffering a vigil sure,
> And plays with childhood in the summer's gold.

But Two Words

His feet refuse no threshold; want and care
Do not repulse Him, nor even sin.
Wherever need is waiting, He is there,
Wherever love invites, He enters in.

(Anon)

Join Me in Jericho

I have no idea where the saying started, but I heard it first from an exasperated schoolmate: "*Go to Jericho!*"

And one day – half a lifetime on – I did! Of my own free will, I'm glad to say, and it turned out to be an unforgettable experience. I had been some time in Jerusalem, the Holy City, set two thousand two hundred feet up above sea level. But almost immediately, the road I set myself to follow dropped away – winding, hazardous, notorious!

I soon realized I owed a lot to Dr Luke, for his account of a happening there. It was one of the Master's stories, which, by the time I actually went to Jericho, had circled the world (Luke 10:30–37; A.V.), though now I feel as certain as ever that it fell with chilling effect on the Master's first hearers.

It started abruptly: "A certain man went down from Jerusalem to Jericho." It was a risky journey at the best of times. Away below sea level it was – one thousand three hundred feet down, with dangerous gorges, *wadis* with caves, and innumerable bends, suggesting hiding places following assault and robbery. The road itself, as the Master's hearers knew well, was called "The Bloody Way". Stones of every possible size were readily to hand, as indeed they are still; weapons for any dastardly deed!

So this poor traveller – "a certain man", who set out as purposefully as any one of us might, to "go to Jericho" – never got there that day! The story goes on to say, as realistically as if it had been in a modern newspaper: "He fell among thieves. And they stripped him, and departed, leaving him half dead."

But that wasn't all, though the Master's hearers must

have sat with their eyebrows raised! It was so real – they had heard of like happenings many a time, among people they knew. They found themselves involved, in a way that I could hardly do, even after I got to Jericho myself. But fortunately, it was a story with a happy ending, thanks to a passer-by. He didn't belong to the same nationality as the injured man, *but he had compassion* – and that was something greatly valued by Dr Luke. And when he came to write the story in his Gospel he didn't forget to say that the man was a Samaritan. He didn't know his name – as he did the names of many of whom he told – but it didn't matter; as the story got passed around, he came to be known as "The Good Samaritan". No one of us could improve on that! Everyone today needs to know that story, which ends up by the traveller, with his little donkey, tending the desperately injured man at the roadside, and carrying him to the safety of a friendly inn. And more than that, he paid his dues and promised more, if it was called for. Unfortunately, I have to admit that compassion of that sort is still rather scarce today in many of the world's "Bloody Ways".

*

But Jericho, as a setting, furnished Dr Luke with yet another memorable story (Luke 18:35), but this time it was the Master Himself who was travelling. "And it came to pass," Luke found himself recording, as strikingly as he did the other story, "that as He was come nigh unto Jericho, a certain blind man sat by the wayside begging." (And having been there myself, I can visualize it: the harsh, gritty, dusty road, the sun beating through in strong shafts, the welcome shade of the palms in places. At the time of which Luke tells, the town was six foot-slogging hours from Jerusalem. One doesn't now need to go toilfully on foot to Jericho. Had transport not been ready to serve, I must have been denied the privilege of going there.)

Blind Bartimaeus, when he sat there by the way, was not

slow to sense that something was astir. He lived by his ears
– "And hearing the multitude pass by," writes Luke, "he
asked what it meant. And they told him, that Jesus of
Nazareth passeth by." (And this story, as I think over it,
seems to me every bit as practical and relevant as the other
that I owe to the same record-keeper; for it underlines the
lovely quality of *Perseverance*, just as the other showed me
the importance of *Compassion*.)

Bartimaeus, ignoring the crowd, was not slow to seize an
opportunity that he might well have awaited for who knows
how long. "He cried, saying, 'Jesus, thou son of David,
have mercy on me.'" He couldn't know that Jesus was on
His way up to face the conflicting passions of Jerusalem,
and would never pass that way again. This, had Bartimaeus
known it, was really the chance of a lifetime. But he did not
need to know as much. For him, it was enough to learn that
any minute Jesus would be no further than an arm's length
away from where he sat in his darkness. Added to that was
news of the wonderful things He had done for others in
trouble.

The Master's disciples must have felt the tension of that
hour. But the crowd cared only to stop Bartimaeus calling
out. It was usual for a Rabbi to teach as he walked, and
Jesus was doing this. Naturally, those near Him wanted to
hear what He was saying, and grew angry, rebuking
Bartimaeus "that he should hold his peace". To them he
was only a nuisance – they were over-used to him sitting
day by day there on the roadside. "But", says Luke, "he
cried so much the more, 'Thou son of David, have mercy
on me.'"

*And his perseverance there that day, earned him what he
so eagerly sought!* To everybody's surprise, there amidst the
crowd, "Jesus stood, and commanded Bartimaeus to be
brought unto Him: and when he was come near, He asked
him, saying, 'What wilt thou that I shall do unto thee?' And
he said, 'Lord, that I may receive my sight.' And Jesus said
unto him, 'Receive thy sight: thy faith hath saved thee.'

"And immediately, he received his sight," Dr Luke was able to add as he concluded his story, "and followed Him, glorifying God: and all the people, when they saw it, gave praise unto God." So both of these Jericho stories that Dr Luke recorded have *a happy ending*: the traveller cruelly beaten and robbed, taken presently to the inn on the Good Samaritan's little donkey, and cared for; and now poor Bartimaeus, at last able to see the blue of the sky above him, the palms, and balsams, and, as part of his surroundings, the massed faces of the milling crowd, singing praises – and more wonderful still, the face of the Master, Jesus, looking straight into his own clear-seeing eyes!

Commenting on this lovely example of the all too rare art of perseverance, Dr William Barclay gave as a heading in a popular study book, "The Perseverance of Bartimaeus". And I'm sure Dr Luke would have accepted that as a title. "No obstacles, no discouragement, could stop this needy man in his darkness – he was not to be deterred. It was his splendid spirit that made it possible for Jesus to heal him."

*

Perseverance, to many today, scarcely seems an attractive quality, but it can issue in praise to God. I recall, with undiminished delight, one English day's ending that brought me to the quietness and beauty of Stoke Poges, in Buckinghamshire. There, I knew myself to be in the setting of Thomas Gray's immortal poem. It was a perfect evening, as I parked my car on the gentle piece of green, in sight of the church, girdled with great trees. With time to spare, I tried to recall his poem:

> The curfew tolls the knell of parting day,
>   The lowing herd winds slowly o'er the lea,
> The ploughman homeward plods his weary way,
>   And leaves the world to darkness and to me.

91

Good Company

Now fades the glimmering landscape on the sight,
    And all the air a solemn stillness holds,
Save where the beetle wheels his droning flight,
    And drowsy tinklings lull the distant folds.

Any pilgrim now to that last resting place of the poet, and the carefully tended grassy graveyard where "the rude forefathers of the hamlet sleep", will surely never forget the privilege, especially one like myself, from the ends of the earth. But few, I believe, will know of the perseverance of the poet. (As a writer, that has challenged me many a time.)

For the glorious truth is that Thomas Gray revised his long poem *seventy-five times* – and all seventy-five versions may still be seen, in the safekeeping of the British Museum in London. There is nothing quite like it. Begun in the summer of 1742, his now-famous poem *was not finished to his own satisfaction, and privately published, until eight years of his life had gone by*!

Living as you and I do, in hasty, speed-loving days, when so many among us are ready to settle for the second best, this is a rebuke – and in the realm of the spirit, a challenge. As are those two lovely Jericho stories given us by Dr Luke, celebrating *Compassion*, and *Perseverance*!

Lost – and Found

As my stay in the populous city of Milan was at an end, I took the airport bus some miles out to my plane. It was a lengthy ride, as such rides go, and a pleasant one.

But when I reported there, with but a few minutes to spare, it was to learn that my baggage was lost. I had handed it over at the bus centre in Milan as instructed. Was it still there, all those miles back? I didn't know; nothing like this had ever happened to me before. So I dashed off to another office I'd noticed as we came in – my travelling companion disappearing on the same search, but in another direction.

Then, over the loudspeaker in an Italian voice came a message: "*The luggage of Snowdonie is found!*"

And I shall never forget that moment! I am not a person who loses things: in my lifetime of travel, they've not added up to more than an umbrella in Oxford and a toothbrush in New York! But this time on my arrival in London I learned how widespread this experience is. That very year just finished, said a newspaper, passengers had lost 361,000 articles on London's buses and undergrounds alone (I should like to have known what the airlines' record was), and that was not counting bikes, cats, dogs, and children. Umbrellas numbered 84,000. In the next week or so, I found myself in one of the big London stores, quietly looking around, when a call came over the air: "We have a little boy in our main office at the moment. He says his name is Timothy, and Timothy's lost! Would the listener concerned, who hears this, please come and collect him!"

This, I am told, goes on all the time in one way or another, not only with children but with adults too! Professor W. E. Hocking underlined it in an address, by saying: "There is more *lostness* in the world today, more widespread, even deliberate lostness than ever before. Progress does not carry with it religious progress. It means rather that men have found new ways of being lost."

*

So three of our Master's stories, recorded by Dr Luke in his Gospel, will never be out of date, if what Professor Hocking says is so. There is, it seems, greater need today than ever before, that we should give attention to them. And wonderful stories they are, listened now to the world round – so simple, and so close to life!

No one better kept His eyes open than Jesus, and He did not forget that the crowds to whom He told His stories were very mixed, but He knew how to hold their interest. "Never man spake like this man", was the report of some hard-headed characters sent out to trap Him. He wasn't the first great teacher to put His message into parables. It was a long-established method; but He showed Himself a master at it.

And dear Dr Luke gathers all three of His best-known parables into one chapter of his Gospel, Luke 15. One concerns an inanimate thing – *a coin*; one, a creature possessed of life – *a sheep*; one – *a young man*, son of a loving father. And of each, the Master Storyteller makes plain two realities: *each is lost, and each is precious*!

Beginning at the lowest level, there is *the coin*, and the woman who lost it. My first and natural thought is that it is a very ordinary thing. But Dr Luke wrote of it: "What woman having ten pieces of silver, if she lose one piece, doth not light a candle, and sweep the house, and seek diligently till she find it? And when she hath found it, she calleth her friends and her neighbours together, saying, Rejoice with me; for I have found the piece which I had lost. Likewise", the story finishes, "I say unto you, there is joy in the presence of the angels of God over one sinner that repenteth" (v. 8; A.V.).

Well, one can't rightly say, after that, that the coin of this little story is too small or commonplace to consider. Not at all. It is true, we don't rightly know now whether it was one of the ten little silver ones that made up the head-dress of a married woman, as was the custom in Palestine; or whether it was a coin of the realm, that had slipped from a poor woman's purse. Some modern scholars think the former, some the latter, but that isn't important – the great thing is that it was lost. For years, one of them tells us, a young girl would scrape and save to amass her ten coins, for the head-dress was almost the equivalent of a wedding ring. When she had it, it was so inalienably hers, that it could not even be taken from her for debt.

But it may have been a silver *drachma* that was lost. If so, it was worth then about nine old pence, a full day's pay for a working husband in Palestine at the time the story was told. No wonder it was precious! And once lost, it would be very hard to find it in a peasant's house, which would be dark at floor level. The floor itself was of hard beaten earth, covered with dried reeds and rushes. To hunt for a coin there would be like looking for our proverbial "needle in a haystack". It didn't really matter much what kind of a coin it was, but this much was certain: it was precious and it was lost. And, to round off the story – *it was found*! Dr R. E. Roberts, in our day, uses a very commonplace illustration to make this real to us: "A penny in your purse excites no interest, but let it roll under the seats in a bus, and the whole complement of passengers will go to endless trouble and perform miracles of contortion to find it. The universe will be wrong until it is discovered and restored to its owner."

*

Then turn a thought to our Master's word picture of *the Lost Sheep*. Another modern scholar, Dr Hugh Martin, says: "Whoever sits down to write about the fifteenth chapter of St Luke's Gospel . . . feels that volumes could do no justice to the wealth that is here displayed. For sheer artistry, this story is among the greatest in the world's literature. It is fascinating. One could willingly dwell on the consummate skill of the character drawing, where every phrase tells, and upon the dramatic fitness of every line. Again, each of these tales is a window into a world of ancient Eastern life that invites the closest examination; and much might be written in explanation. Yet again, each chapter reveals the mind of Jesus, the friend of publicans and sinners, so that whole books might be written on that theme alone with these words as text. These stories are revolutionary in their revelation of the nature of the Eternal God . . .

"A thing is 'lost' when its owner is deprived of the proper use and enjoyment of it. A coin is lost when it cannot be used as coinage, or as ornament. A sheep is lost when it has strayed away from the care and control of its shepherd." So we turn to the word picture of *the lost sheep*. "And He spake this parable unto them, saying, What man of you, having an hundred sheep, if he lose one of them, doth not leave the ninety and nine in the wilderness, and go after that which is lost, until he find it? And when he hath found it, he layeth it on his shoulders, rejoicing. And when he cometh home, he calleth together his friends and neighbours, saying unto them, Rejoice with me; for I have found my sheep which was lost.

"I say unto you", adds the Supreme Storyteller, "that likewise joy shall be in heaven over one sinner that repenteth, more than over ninety and nine just persons, which need no repentance" (Luke 15:3–7; A.V.).

*

The coin has its value, and the sheep has its value, but it is when we move into the area of the third story, the one we call "The Prodigal Son", that the value heightens and deepens into the realm of Love. It is hardly necessary, perhaps, to copy out the Gospel account of it – most of us know it off by heart – but it will serve to refresh our minds. Dr Luke's words, beginning at verse 11, are: "A certain man had two sons: and the younger of them said to his father, Father, give me the portion of goods that falleth to me. And he divided unto them his living. And not many days after, the younger son gathered all together, and took his journey into a far country, and there wasted his substance with riotous living.

"And when he had spent all, there arose a mighty famine in that land: and he began to be in want. And he went and joined himself to a citizen of that country; and he sent him into his fields to feed swine. And he would fain have filled his belly with the husks that the swine did eat; and no man gave unto him.

"And when he came to himself, he said, How many hired servants of my father's have bread enough and to spare, and I perish with hunger. I will arise and go to my father, and will say unto him, Father, I have sinned against heaven, and before thee. And am no more worthy to be called thy son: make me as one of thy hired servants.

"And he arose, and came to his father. But when he was yet a great way off, his father saw him, and had compassion, and ran, and fell on his neck, and kissed him. And the son said unto him, Father, I have sinned against heaven, and in thy sight, and am no more worthy to be called thy son.

"But the father said to his servants, Bring forth the best robe, and put it on him; and put a ring on his hand, and shoes on his feet: and bring hither the fatted calf, and kill it; and let us eat, and be merry: For this my son was dead, and is alive again: *he was lost, and is found*. And they began to be merry." (But this isn't the end of the story . . .)

"Now his elder son was in the field: and as he came and drew nigh to the house, he heard music and dancing. And he called one of the servants, and asked what these things meant. And he said unto him, Thy brother is come; and thy father hath killed the fatted calf, because he hath received him safe and sound.

"And he was angry, and would not go in: therefore came his father out, and intreated him. And he answering said to his father, Lo, these many years do I serve thee, neither transgressed I at any time thy commandment: and yet thou never gavest me a kid, that I might make merry with my friends: But as soon as this thy son was come, which hath devoured thy living with harlots, thou hast killed for him the fatted calf.

"And he said unto him, Son, thou art ever with me, and all that I have is thine. It was meet that we should make merry, and be glad: for this thy brother was dead, and is alive again; and *was lost and is found*."

Dr Shafto says clearly for us: "The Prodigal does wrong, and comes to realize it; but the Elder son is wrong . . . and does not see it. The Prodigal recognizes that to be a servant is as much as he has any right to expect; but the Elder son has always been a servant, and not a son in spirit." It was when I saw this as clearly as I do now that I summed it up in "Two Lost Sons".

> Pig's-wash of wild husks was one's bread,
> with poor rags to cover his back,
> while his brother ate well, and wore
> fine linen with a bright golden thread;
> but both were prodigals – apart,
> one, in the sad "far country",
> one, at home, dark with resentment
> eating deep into his heart.
>
> (R.F.S.)

It is possible still, to be "lost" – and "found" – anywhere!

John Burroughs felt that he had to pass on the words of a worshipper he knows in a certain church: "I come here to find myself; *it is so easy to get lost in the world*!"

Fragments

I don't often hear the word these days, but it's one of my favourites. It belongs to my happy childhood, to my very earliest schooldays. There wasn't much money about in those times and we learned not to look for presents. When our father had business to do, which wasn't very often, he would harness Old Jack to the family trap, and set off. We could expect him back from the town about our bedtime, "clop clopping" over the quiet country road that brought him again to our gate. (It was years before I learned that the distance was thirteen miles each way – it seemed then that the two of them, greatly loved, had been on a great adventure.)

In time, our mother joined our father – and then things took a turn that quickened expectation, as we waited for them at night. By then we had settled into going to school, and on our way home in the mid-afternoon we stayed with a near neighbour, Miss Evelyn Palmer, till our parents could pick us up. That was an event for us twins. Hitherto, our town-going presents had had to be bought – and our father knew that he wasn't expected to spend much on them. He might stretch to two pence, for a penny pencil each; or buy us each a banana; or a "Tobler chocolate" all the way from Switzerland.

But there was a joint present every now and again, that rejoiced our young hearts beyond anything that we'd known till then. *It was a gift of fragments* that didn't cost anything, though it was years before we could take this in. The simple and surprising truth was that our mother, before her marriage, had a special friend who went off to a dressmaker's establishment to learn the skills imparted there. Our mother, I imagine now, didn't see much of her in those years, but by letter, and an occasional visit when she had moved to her own little place of business, the long-time friendship held. And how glad we children were about that! For on those all too rare town days, when she was able to accompany our father and Old Jack, a call was always made on the homeward journey.

On those happy occasions, there would always be a cup of tea waiting, though their stay could only be brief. And there was always a bag of "fragments". Sometimes it was a real *bag* – a paper hat-bag, gloriously spacious; but when she hadn't one, an old pillowcase served.

Inside – saved up for us – there were wonderful "fragments": bits of silk, pieces of gay ribbon, odd scraps of velvet of one colour or another, too small to be useful in a grown-ups' dressmaking establishment, but just the thing to quicken wonder in the eyes and heart of any little girl-mother for her dollies! Odd shapes and sizes, those "fragments", but of wonderful colours! And all mixed up! But just the thing, with the help of our mother, to engage us for hours, and to rig out our country dollies to the smartness of any in town!

So the word "fragments" slipped into my excited heart and imagination. And you'll not be surprised to hear of my delight, in adulthood, to find that word four times over in my New Testament, telling of a miraculous happening. And it's still set firmly in my affection, as I read of that picnic recorded in Matthew 14:20; in Mark 6:43; in Luke 9:17; and in John 6:12.

Ever since my visit to Palestine, it has been easier for me to visualize the scene. I continue to be struck by the fact that it is the *only* miracle recorded in all four Gospels. There must be a reason for that!

That it occurred just when it did, is certainly significant, for it gives an impressive picture of the spirit of our Lord. His Twelve had just then come back from a special period of ministry. They had things they wanted to tell Him; and He, without doubt, could have welcomed the opportunity, just as much, to be alone with them. To that end, He had taken them to a quiet place, in the neighbourhood of Bethsaida, which was a village on the far side of the Jordan, to the north of the Sea of Galilee.

But, alas, it was not to be, that purposeful and refreshing Retreat! News of where He had gone with His disciples, reached the people, and caring only for their own interests, they surged out in a determined crowd to that very spot. And incredible as it may seem to some of us who in our own day have had the responsibility of planning a retreat of any sort, we have Dr Luke reporting that "He received them", or as Dr Barclay interpreted those words for modern times, "*He welcomed them.*" Imagine it! Imagine yourself in such a situation, and then realize, as you must, that there were five thousand of them! You might expect to be forgiven your poor spirit, if you were a bit "scratchy"; at least, it would be understandable. But Jesus welcomed them! He "spake unto them of the Kingdom of God, and healed them that had need of healing" – which was what they'd come for.

And seeing that the day was wearing towards its close, He went on to show concern for their physical comfort. The best that the twelve disciples could say, was: "Send the crowd away!" But He knew that they were hungry people, and a long way from home or from any village where they could get food. After suggesting that together they should undertake to feed them, He made the very practical suggestion that they should be seated there on the ground, just where they were, in little groups of fifties. Mark takes pleasure in referring to "the green grass" where they were. It makes a nice picture, as they relaxed in their many-coloured garments, like a series of flowerbeds!

Then the miracle that only Christ could work, happened – and don't say that I am writing off its wonder, only say (I quote Dr Barclay) that it was an unexpected wonder. Just a few loaves and fishes, to feed all that crowd! "The people were hungry", says Dr Barclay reverently, "*and utterly selfish.* They all had something with them, but they would not even produce it for themselves in case they had to share it with others. Jesus took the five loaves and the two fishes and looked up into heaven and blessed them, and broke them, and gave them to His disciples to set before the crowd. Thereupon others were moved to produce their little store, and in the end there was more than enough for everyone. So it may be regarded as a miracle which turned selfish, suspicious folk into generous people, a miracle of what happens when, moved by Christ, people are moved to share."

And here we come to the loveliest verse: "And when they were filled, He said unto His disciples, *Gather up the fragments* . . . that nothing be lost!" (John 6:12).

*

And those words of our Master and Lord come ringing down on us today, as we handle food in a hungry world! And in other areas of our life, too!

Many knowing me and my dedication to Christian service for a long time, ask how I manage to do so much, read so much, write so many books. If I share my answer – without any hint of boasting, as it always is – I have to own to being a disciplined person, a hard-working person. But there are many of those. My chief answer, I think, is with "the fragments", the left-over, odd bits of time. We all have them. Our loss is in not knowing what to do with them – or even, indeed, that we can do anything with them. From the beginning, we fall so easily to telling ourselves, and any others who show themselves interested, that *there isn't time*! But that, of course, is an old excuse. Paul had occasion to thrash it out with some of his friends among the early Christians of Ephesus. And his words, translated for us in Phillips's New Testament, have a strong, eager, sensible ring: "*Make the best use of your time, despite all the difficulties of these days*" (Ephesians 5:16).

It's fun enough, as children, to learn by heart the little

poem dear youthful-spirited Eleanor Farjeon wrote for her child-friends:

There isn't time, there isn't time
To do the things I want to do,
With all the mountain-tops to climb,
And all the woods to wander through,
And all the seas to sail upon,
And everywhere there is to go,
And all the people, every one
Who lives upon the earth, to know.
There's only time, there's only time
To know a few, and do a few,
And then sit down and make a rhyme
About the rest I want to do.

Very charming for a child, and to a considerable degree true! But we adults ought to have discovered that it's foolish to imagine that we can do everything! We can't! But we can do much by using our "fragments" of time!

"If I could be sure that people have a right habit with reference to fragments of time," said that choice Christian spirit in our day, Dr John R. Mott, with whom I talked at the Oxford World Conference, "I wouldn't worry about what they do with the large portions."

And I know what he means!

The writer Evelyn Richardson astonished me with what she did with "the fragments", beyond her busy schedule during World War II, when she helped to look after a lighthouse. A few minutes at a time were all she ever had, but she gathered them up, and nothing was lost.

A worthwhile secret!

Thankful Hearts

Year by year, in our little Chapel at Harvest Festival time, in the beautiful countryside where I grew up, we could be sure of a crowded congregation. Everybody came – and one year, that nobody ever forgets, a big pig came too. That only happened once, fortunately. Old Geordie Miller next door, who owned the creature, allowed it to root about in a rough piece of orchard near his home, from time to time.

One Saturday, when several of us responsible for gathering up sheaves, apples, grapes, pumpkins, and all the rest that made up our Harvest Festival, had set everything in place, the little Chapel had to be safely locked till the next afternoon. Being full autumn, it was very warm and fragrant when the door was next opened, and the congregation poured in. No sooner had our service begun, than the same accumulation of harvest fragrances, it seemed, reached Geordie Miller's old pig that became aware of them and followed them, finding his way up the polished aisle. Now, you may not know – as many of us did not, until that moment, when two of our stewards rose to lay hold of it, and pull it out – that a pig is not built to reverse. Its little trotters stuck into the lino up the aisle. There was nothing for it but to hold it steady, whilst two other worshippers from the front seats removed sheaves, and prize marrows, apples and other items, and made room to take the pig forward – where it wanted to go – and turn it round in the space now provided, and together take it back down to the door, and out. That incident was never to be forgotten.

Nor was our hearty singing that belonged to Thanksgiving, season by season. Old Geordie Miller took good care to lock up his pig after that, but nothing ever happened to lock up our singing.

You will understand how delighted I was to come upon a country Harvest Festival experience in Anne Treneer's charming book *School House in the Wind*. Her family lived in Cornwall, in a small community where her father was the schoolmaster. "By September", she wrote years afterwards, happily looking back, as I've just looked back to our Harvest, "the village was ready to praise God for the harvest. Sometimes we praised Him too soon, and sang that all was safely gathered in, before it was. But we knew that God would understand. No need to explain to Him that the day for the Harvest Festival had been fixed some weeks ago . . . Men seemed to come together with more willingness to express praise and gratitude than to bewail their sins, and consider how fearful it was to fall into the hands of the living God. People went round to different parishes to Harvest Festivals, and Chapel went to Church and Church people went to Chapel", said Anne Treneer. "We did not seem to mind how often we sang 'We plough the fields and scatter', 'Now thank we all our God', 'Come, ye thankful people, come', 'For His mercies still endure, ever faithful, ever sure', and 'All people that on earth do dwell, Sing to the Lord with cheerful voice'. The first time we ever chanted a psalm in my memory in Gorran church was at a Harvest Festival. Usually we said the psalms, the Vicar reading one verse and the congregation the next, and so on to the end when we sang a Gloria. But for one Harvest Festival we chanted '*O praise God in His Holiness; praise Him in the firmament of His power*'. By the time we reached '*Let everything that hath breath praise the Lord*', I had got the hang of it (as a small child) and was so loud in praise that Mr Jorey, the blacksmith who shod our pony, and who would let us blow the bellows, turned round and gave me a peppermint."

I understand that perfectly, though I've always thought it a pity that anything or anyone should stop people singing praises! It was so when our Lord made His way up into Jerusalem for the last time, as Dr Luke tells of it, unforgettably: "And it came to pass, when He was come nigh to Bethphage and Bethany, at the mount called the mount of Olives, He sent two of His disciples, saying, Go ye into the village over against you; in the which at your entering ye shall find a colt tied, whereon yet never man sat: loose him, and bring him hither. And if any man ask you, Why do ye loose him? thus shall ye say unto him, Because the Lord hath need of him.

"And they that were sent went their way, and found even as He had said unto them. And as they were loosing the colt, the owners thereof said unto them, Why loose ye the colt? And they said, The Lord hath need of him. And they brought him to Jesus: and they cast their garments upon the colt, and they set Jesus thereon. And as He went, they spread their clothes in the way.

"And when He was come nigh, even now at the descent of the mount of Olives, the whole multitude of the disciples began to rejoice and praise God with a loud voice for all the mighty works that they had seen: saying, Blessed be the King that cometh in the name of the Lord: peace in heaven, and glory in the highest. And some of the Pharisees from among the multitude said unto Him, Master, rebuke Thy disciples. And he answered and said unto them, I tell you that, if these should hold their peace, the stones would immediately cry out" (Luke 19:29–40; A.V.).

Jesus knew full well that there were times when Praise to God was the only fitting thing. He had been brought up on the Old Testament scriptures, and there the psalmist had sung:

> Praise the Lord!
> Praise the Lord, O my soul!
> I will praise the Lord as long as I live;
> I will sing praises to my God while I have being!
> (Psalm 146:1–2; R.S.V.)

All through the Book of Psalms, men and women are
exhorted to *Praise God*! From end to end, in their services
and alone, they are to be caught up in a glad "crescendo
of Praise". Countless times, the words recur: "Praise ye the
Lord!" "Praise the Lord!" are the words with which Psalm
147 (R.S.V.) opens:

> For it is good to sing praises to our God;
> For He is gracious, and a song of praise is seemly.

And when the time came in worship that many chose to
sing hymns instead of psalms, there were any number of
gifted souls to lead us, with the mediaeval Jewish Doxology
to bridge us over, as it appears in the Methodist Hymn
Book which I use every Sunday:

> Praise to the living God!
>   All praised be His name,
> Who was, and is, and is to be,
>   For aye the same!
>   The One Eternal God
>   Ere aught that now appears:
> The First, the Last, beyond all thought,
>   His timeless years!
>
>
> Formless, all lovely forms
>   Declare His loveliness;
> Holy, no holiness of earth
>   Can His express.
>   Lo, He is Lord of all!
>   Creation speaks His praise,
> And everywhere, above, below,
>   His will obeys.

Eternal life hath He
   Implanted in the soul;
His love shall be our strength and stay,
   While ages roll.
   Praise to the living God!
   All praises be His name,
Who was, and is, and is to be,
   For aye the same! Amen.

We praise Him, first of all, for what He is in Himself; then for what He has done in creation – in giving us this earth, and its harvests; but more than that: for what He has done for us, in redemption, through Christ, His Son, our Lord; and for His daily, ongoing watchful care! In the spirit of the psalmist (146):

We will praise the Lord as long as we live;
We will sing praises to our God while we have any breath!

And no one will gainsay us, while this life lasts, any more than they did on the day of our Lord's entry into Jerusalem; or on the Harvest Festival day in Cornwall, when a worshipper seated in front of a little girl singing her heart out thought that a peppermint would do it!

For in every way that we know, this life is not only reaching out to our fellows; but up to God!

A Good Word for Martha

I have only ever had one friend by the name of Martha. A splendid, practical Christian she was – and a wonderful cook! I was often a guest in her home, a country manse, shared with her Albert. Born and grown up in England, they married, and came out to my home country after the First World War. Many a one in the service of the Church blessed God for Martha! (I wonder whether any little child anywhere today is ever given that well-known New Testament name? I doubt it – though "Mary", the name of her sister, is one of the most popular.)

Mid-morning, I paused in my work to lend an ear to a man who was pleased to tell me that this fresh August day was specially set aside in his Catholic church to honour *Saint Martha*. And it was good hearing! I have many times, over the years, tried to say "a good word for Martha", but have always felt my effort a somewhat solitary one. But I shall never feel that way again, I am thankful to say.

Martha, of course, has long held her place in Luke's Gospel (10:38–42). The hospitality of the little Bethany home that she shared with her sister, Mary, and their brother, Lazarus, meant much to our Lord. The door was not only constantly "on the latch", as the saying goes, but it was conveniently near to Jerusalem. Nothing now, of course, remains of that little house, save the fragrant memory of it in the Gospels. But I was glad to make a special visit out from the Holy City to its airy setting, when I had the opportunity. (A few new stone houses, I was interested to see, were being built there, no great distance from where a modern road takes its travellers down to distant Amman, capital of Jordan these days. One can only hope that the gracious spirit of that original little home, where Martha presided, can be established there, too.)

As Arthur Feslier was pleased to recount this morning, "She appears in Scripture in the episode where she claims she is overworked in the kitchens. 'Why', she asks, 'doesn't Mary come to give me a hand, instead of sitting at our Guest's feet?'

"Many of us practical people, of course – reading what He replied – feel that He was too harsh. 'Martha, Martha,' He said, 'you worry and fret about so many things. And yet, few are needed – indeed, only one. It is Mary who has chosen the better part. And it shall not be taken from her.'

Well, somehow, as my guest this morning went on boldly, "I think that in making their various translations, some of the scholars have got it a bit mixed. What the Lord was pointing out, was that we don't need many things to live properly and well – least of all, many dishes of food. In fact, only one thing is essential – that is to listen to the word of God, and be guided by it. It is better to do this than to get fussed about worldly affairs. (And that's a message that keeps popping up again and again, in the New Testament.) Even so," Arthur Feslier felt he had to add, "we can sympathize with Martha's point of view, and imagine how she felt: 'That's all very well, but You still have to eat, and I still have to do the dishes.'

"Perhaps the episode reveals that in Martha, you and I see someone who reflects *us*, more than Mary does. It's natural to get a bit petulant when others in the family don't seem to be doing much. And with these two women, Martha was the one who *did* things.

"Have you noticed, that in the chapter about the raising of Lazarus, Martha was the one up and about, while Mary was . . . well, contemplating? There, we read, quite clearly (John 11:5), that 'Jesus loved Martha' (she's named) and He loved her sister and Lazarus, too. Mary remained sitting in the house. Martha talked to Jesus for a moment – and it was after these words, that He said to Martha: '*I* am the Resurrection and the Life.' (Everlasting words!)

"Then Martha went back to Mary, and whispered that the Master wanted to see her. And only then did Mary get up and go to Him – thus missing the great and permanent message of Christian hope. Perhaps she felt a bit embarrassed, and negligent, because it says that she 'arose *quickly*' (v. 29; A.V.). Her reaction was that of a demonstrably emotional person: she threw herself at the Lord's feet (v. 32), down there in the dust, and wept. And, *Jesus wept* (and that's the shortest verse in the Bible). Two powerful, memorable words, full of compassion and love.

"Once again, the practical Martha emerges in this narrative", I was reminded. "When Jesus told someone to take away the stone from Lazarus's tomb. Down-to-earth Martha then told how her brother had been dead for four days . . . And once again, the Lord felt He had to chide her: 'Haven't I told you that if you believe, you'll see the glory of God?' (Even knowing the drama He was involved in, Jesus takes time to remonstrate with Martha.) I wonder how she felt?" queried Arthur Feslier, sympathetically, "because there were lots of people standing about at the time, and no one likes to be put down in public, even mildly. But chided like that," he added, "she took it with humility, I think." (We have no help at all, from Dr Luke, at this point, and little enough from St John – did they find it too painful to register permanently?)

"Let me quote something from another saint, a woman, Teresa of Avila – what she wrote about Martha", added Arthur Feslier: "Martha was holy . . . what more do you want than to be able to be like that woman, worthy to receive the Lord so often in her house . . . to serve Him . . . ? If she had been absorbed as Mary was, there would have been no one to prepare for the Guest . . . *Humility consists in being ready for what the Lord desires.*

"What I like best about this Bible narrative", finished the speaker to whom I listened so appreciatively, "is that our Lord took time to scold a little the very one He loved

111

so dearly. And that despite gentle slaps on the wrist, Martha's love didn't diminish at all. *She learned, and accepted* . . .

"You and I can take heart in this!"

*

Temperament, although such a good gift, I found myself thinking later, cannot be allowed to dominate. It must be subject to discipline, in devoted service. Our discipleship must be *expressed in a beautiful balance*. This, I am certain, we can learn from these two beloved women! They appear again, and finally, tendering a supper to our Lord at Bethany (John 12). "But a comparison between this passage and Luke 10", says a respectful commentator, "shows, indeed, the same Martha, but now there is no record of her over-anxiety or distraction, or of any complaint of her sister's absorption in devotion to the Saviour."

She had by this time, I like to think, laid hold of a glorious sense of proportion, of balance!

I used to like a little poem-prayer – offered by somebody of our day, *as an excuse* – but I don't any more:

> Lord of all pots and pans and things,
>   Since I've no time to be
> A saint by doing lovely things,
>   Or watching late with Thee,
> Or dreaming in the dawnlight,
>   Or storming heaven's gates,
> Make me a saint by getting meals
>   And washing up the plates.
>
> (Anon)

Saint Martha, I am sure, can teach us better than that!

So Much for Miracles

We always had a good garden around the home where I grew up, and I loved it, back to the morning when my mother said to me as a little child, "Shut your eyes, and open your hand, and see what God will send you!"

And I did. Next moment, when I opened my eyes and looked in the palm of my little hand, there was something there. "What is it?" I asked. And she said: "A miracle!" In the next moment I saw that it was little seeds, a tiny pile of them, and I was instructed how to plant them. In time, they became little green shoots, and a long time afterwards – or so it seemed to me in my waiting – they showed little bright blue daisy faces, and got the name Michaelmas daisies. And I've been interested in seeds, ever since.

When I got a kindly present – *A Book of Town Verse*, published by the Oxford University Press – I was an adult, with lots of world travel behind me, but still the fascination of "miracles" held me – their "God-givenness", their colour and shape. And I recalled the first time I held out my hand to receive such things, for in that little book, of a size to slip into my pocket, I found a poem called "The Seed Shop", by Muriel Stuart. I had never heard of her, but soon I could see that we were kindred spirits. She wrote:

> Here in a quiet and dusty room they lie,
> Faded as crumbled stone or shifting sand,
> Forlorn as ashes, shrivelled, scentless, dry –
> Meadows and gardens running through my hand.

Good Company

In this brown husk a dale of hawthorn dreams,
A cedar in this narrow cell is thrust
That will drink deeply of a century's streams,
These lilies shall make summer on my dust.

Here in their safe and simple house of death,
Sealed in their shells a million roses leap;
Here I can blow a garden with my breath,
And in my hand a forest lies asleep.

*

In my first week in London during my first visit to that city
of countless shops, I found my way to a seedshop, and went
to Kew Gardens. Very fittingly, it was early spring, and the
world of countless seeds was coming alive. Kew, of course,
is a wonderful place, and I have never failed to go there
again whenever I've been in London. It's like a great park
of miracles – seeds, plants and trees as you will know, if
you've ever been there. My guidebook does its best to
minister to my wonder. "The prime function of the Royal
Botanic Gardens it says, is the correct identification of
plants. For this purpose, the scientific staff have at their
disposal a Herbarium, containing over six million sheets of
dried specimens. In the Gardens themselves between
45,000 and 50,000 different kinds of plants are cultivated
. . ." Imagine it! "The visitor", it adds, "may wander at will
through what is practically a lordly park, of nearly three
hundred acres, with every species of tree, shrub and flower
plainly labelled for his edification. The grounds comprise
stately avenues and sequestered walks, lakes and ponds,
palm-houses and conservatories, gorgeous flower beds,
rockeries, museums and classic temples, and a large
herbaceous ground . . ." Imagine it! But you can't,
especially in spring! It adds up to *a multitude of miracles* –
with my guidebook going on to speak of Kew's ministry in
raising from gathered seeds, essential plants at one time
unknown, giving us Brazil rubber and the quinine

plants from South America.

But what I always like, no distance in from the gate by which I have again and again chosen to enter, is a fine figure of a Sower, with his bag of seed slung over his shoulder. He is a lithe, lovely figure, made to represent involvement in one of the most exciting and hopeful undertakings on earth – just sowing seed. I remember my own father, as a young man, before ever he shared a mechanical seed-drill with a neighbour, striding hopefully up and down a field he sowed every year, just beyond the hedge surrounding our home-garden. And it gave me joy! The generous swing of his arm, as he plunged his hand into his seedbag, and swung it widely, was wonderful. It must have been this kind of action that attracted Jesus to the sower of whom He told, going up and down a nearby field, perhaps even as He told His parable. And when he came to write his Gospel, Dr Luke delighted to tell of it.

And there was a relevance and freshness about his words. "A sower went out to sow his seed: and as he sowed, some fell by the wayside: and it was trodden down, and the fowls of the air devoured it. And some fell upon a rock: and as soon as it was sprung up, it withered away, because it lacked moisture. And some fell among thorns: and the thorns sprang up with it, and choked it. And others fell on good ground, and sprang up, *and bare fruit an hundredfold.*" (A very hopeful climax!)

"And when He had said these things, He cried, He that hath ears to hear, let him hear. And His disciples asked Him, saying, What might this parable be? And He said, Unto you it is given to know the mysteries of the Kingdom of God . . . Now the parable is this: *The seed is the word of God.* Those by the wayside are they that hear; then cometh the devil, and taketh away the word out of their hearts, lest they should believe and be saved. They on the rock are they, which, when they hear, receive the word with joy; and these have no root, which for a while believe, and in time of temptation fall away. And that which fell among thorns are they, which, when they have heard, go forth, and are choked with cares and riches and pleasures of this life, and bring no fruit to perfection. But that on the good ground are they, which in an honest and good heart, having heard the word, keep it, and bring forth fruit with patience." (Another lovely, hopeful climax!)

To His disciples' query He answered: "*The seed is the word of God.*"

This, it seemed plain to me as I stood in the entry of the British and Foreign Bible Society buildings in London, as their guest to lunch, and an examination of the glorious Library there, was the reality responsible for their striking "Sower" window. Standing freely, his seedbag hung over his shoulder, he moves purposefully, with his arm outstretched, sowing! It takes one back to the words of the Master, in His parable, and the comment of my long-time friend, Dr William Barclay: "Jesus speaks this parable and in it He is saying, 'Every farmer knows that some of his seed will be lost; it cannot all grow. But that does not discourage him or make him stop sowing, because he knows that in spite of that, the harvest is sure.' It is Jesus saying to His disciples, '*I know we have our setbacks and our discouragements; I know we have our enemies and our opponents; but never despair; in the end the harvest is sure!*'"

*

Those of us who here and now serve His Kingdom – missionaries, ministers, medical men and women like those to whom this book is dedicated, writers, teachers, and the rest of us set to countless other "sowings" for His sake – are understandably interested in seeds, both *in the natural sense, and in the spiritual*. William Carey, the great, eager founder of modern missions, offers proof of this; seeds of any sort were to him of God's making, and symbols of rich beauty and fulfilment. Toiling away in India, he wrote home to those who cared for God's creation, material and spiritual: "Give a boy a penny a day to gather seeds of cowslips and daisies . . . Send every kind. I shall be glad of the smallest. Think none insignificant."

Our Lord told us of "the mustard seed" – to the same end, of encouraging us even in our smallest "sowings". And some of them do seem small in our comings and goings – a word here; a cup of cold water there, by way of refreshment; a loan of a book we've liked; a lift in the car to some devotional gathering; a neighbourly phonecall in a time of illness or anxiety. Or it might be a funny little story that has occasioned laughter in the family; a piece of good news just to hand. Whatever it is, however small, sow it for the sake of Christ, in some soil that will welcome it!

"Gordon's Tomb" in Jerusalem is a nice quiet garden to visit and beautifully set, with its wall-tomb, tree-blessed. I'm glad I was able to spend an hour there. Some think of it as the tomb in which our Lord's body was lain. Others are as confident that it couldn't be, being too far from the city wall.

As I was leaving, the gardener asked me to hold out my hand, and when I did, he placed there a few seeds, proverbial for smallness. Our Lord once spoke of such but I had never seen the like before – and they will never now be forgotten. Mustard seed! The tiniest seed I've ever seen; and often due to grow to more than the full height of two tall men!

So much for miracles!

Troubadours of God

I can remember clearly my impression of the first missionary I ever set eyes upon, when I was a small girl, and that she came from Persia. She captured our whole-hearted interest, having some nice things to show us and some nice things to tell us.

I don't know whether any of my friends have – in maturity – ever managed to visit that far-away land to which she introduced us. It has never been my privilege to travel that way, despite all the many journeys I have made. But I have visited Jerusalem, and established very strong friendships with missionaries there, where Christian missions first started at the word of our Lord and Master, Risen and Ascended!

And all over that little land – reaching out ever further, as did those whom He first commissioned – I have been well received, and have shared the very wonderful things we have in common, as in many other lands, too! Sunday by Sunday, now that I am home, I sit at worship immediately behind one greying missionary couple, and immediately in front of another, likewise retired from outstanding service in the British Solomon Islands.

Dr Luke would be honoured, I feel sure, to sit in pew-space that either of these missionary couples would make for him; as indeed I would be greatly honoured to have him sit where I sit, in the pew between them. He would be at ease with us, for we often read from his Gospel, and his "Acts of the Apostles", rejoicing in the fact that even his Gospel, as Dr James S. Stewart reminds us today, "is a missionary Gospel, and that the Christ it portrays is not primarily the Messiah of Israel at all, but the Saviour of the whole earth . . . Moreover, the missionary motive was

obviously, for Luke, the deciding factor in determining
which incidents and parables, out of all the mass of material
at his disposal, he should include. In this connection", Dr
Stewart adds, "it is only necessary to mention the Parable
of the Good Samaritan; the incident of the one grateful
leper (17:11 'and he was a Samaritan'); and such sayings of
Jesus as, 'They shall come from *the east*, and from *the west*,
and from *the north*, and from *the south*, and shall sit down
in the Kingdom of God' (13:29). *It is pre-eminently the
Gospel of a universal hope.*" Dr William Barclay – jointly
honoured with Dr Stewart for their long ministry, some
while ago at a fine gathering in Scotland – was struck by this
same fact. "All the Gospel writers", said he, "begin by
quoting Isaiah 40:3. Only Luke continues the passage to
include the saying: '*All flesh shall see the salvation of God*'"
(Matthew 3:3; Mark 1:2–3; John 1:23; Luke 3:4–
6).

In his lifetime – the early days of missionaries, when
there were few to know, besides Paul – Luke knew them!
Sometimes, no doubt, some of them looked a bit shabby
and travel-worn, as have some even in our time, though
that was not part of my earliest picture of a missionary,
since it was a bright, national costume that she wore.

My English friend of more recent times, dear Pauline
Webb, who has travelled widely in the interest of missions,
even to my own distant country, introduced me to a letter
from a London newspaper, claiming to underline the
difference between an American woman and a British
woman. The writer of the letter quoted one American
woman as saying: "There goes a missionary. I must buy her
a new hat!" But when a British woman, she contended,
sees a missionary, she says: "There goes a missionary, I
must buy myself a new hat, and give her my old one!"

I chuckled; but perhaps I ought not to have done so. I
have no experience that would lead me to believe it.
Certainly, it wasn't true in Dr Luke's day, that the second-
best was good enough for missions, and missionaries.

Then, missions called for the very best that any of the
followers of the Risen Christ had to offer. And, in reality,
it is still the same today. That means: *"Sharing the faith we
know; knowing the faith we share!"*

It is not easy to describe a modern-day missionary, nor
a modern-day giver to missions. It goes so much deeper
than a matter of hats – if it comes to that, many, the world
round, don't wear hats. And missionaries are still
wholehearted men and women, and better turned out than
they have ever been, in every way. Somebody, in *World
Outlook*, a modern journal, and so fittingly titled,
asked:

Who are these
That run along the highways of the world?
That seek its meanest suburbs with their feet?
They are *the troubadours of God*.
Blowing an airy melody along earth's aisles
As solid as the masonry of dreams.
They are the wise eccentrics
Who reason with divine hilarity.
They are the canny merchants
Who buy the hearts of nations for their Prince.
They are the vivid tailors
Who push the threads of ages through their hands.
They are the white militia
Who take no blood, to spill it, save their own.
They are the blessed coolies
Who lift the loads of folly on their backs
And dump them into truth's dissolving streams.
They are the blithe outrunners
Who trek the world's long reaches for old trails
Whereon to lay the pavement of new years.
They are the grave cross-carriers
Who bear stern wooden gibbets on their backs
And nail their loves and treasures to the beams.
They are our princely brothers,

Born of the womb which bore us,
Who speak for us amid the courts of life.

Don't refuse to accept the reality of this just because it's
poetry. How else can one begin to set down things of the
spirit? The psalmists knew no better way and so they wrote
in poetry and song! And Luke found himself setting down
in his Gospel, the song of Mary, the young mother of our
Lord, the *Magnificat*, because *she sees herself honoured to
be in God's service*! How else can the deepest experiences
of the spirit be expressed? Mary said – according to Luke
1:46; A.V. – "My soul doth magnify the Lord. And my
spirit hath rejoiced in God, my Saviour. For He hath
regarded the low estate of His handmaiden; for, behold,
from henceforth all generations shall call me blessed. For
He that is mighty hath done to me great things; and holy
is His name. And His mercy is on them that fear Him, from
generation to generation. He hath shewed strength with
His arm; He hath scattered the proud in the imagination
of their hearts. He hath put down the mighty from their
seats, and exalted them of low degree. He hath filled the
hungry with good things; and the rich He hath sent empty
away. He hath holpen His servant Israel, in remembrance
of His mercy. As He spake to our fathers, to Abraham, and
to his seed for ever!

"And Mary abode with Elizabeth about three months,
and returned to her own house."

Of course, it's not always poetry at home, any more than
it is always poetry on the mission field. Far from it! The
Anglican Diocese of Polynesia is on record as having once
advertised for a missionary, to match a certain
opportunity. But not in poetry, in the following words: "A
candidate must have the ability to mix with people – also
to mix concrete; to wade rivers; to write articles; to love
one's neighbour; to deliver babies; to sit cross-legged; to
conduct meetings; to drain swamps; to digest questionable
dishes; to patch up human weaknesses; to suffer fools

gladly; and to burn the midnight oil.

"Any person allergic to ants, beggars, chop suey, cockroaches, curried crabs, duplicators, guitars, humidity, itches, jungles, mildew, and poverty, sweat, and unmarried mothers, had better think twice before applying."

Realism, you say? Yes, but the spirit of missionary living and giving of one's self, that can be beautifully, poetically expressed, is often not a whit less practical. Countless Christians of every nationality, the world around, find themselves called to live amongst people with habits and history far removed from their own, with a community future utterly different, and, before they can be of any use, a language that must be learned. But in no time, they manage to learn from them, as well as teach them, with that lovely spirit called *respect*, and at its very deepest, *love*!

The word "Missionary" at one time meant for most people a preacher, a teacher, a doctor, a nurse – and that's all. But someone seeking to serve on the mission field today might be heard to say, "I can't preach, but I'm a qualified drainage engineer"; or "I have no training as a teacher, but I'm an experienced motorman, and could look after your boats." And that would be good news on many a mission station! Other volunteers with no nursing training or experience might offer as dieticians; or find a needy service as book-keepers. Each of them, in the mission hospital or out of it, would be as surely motivated by a deep Christian desire to help, to extend, and to serve the Kingdom of God on earth.

It Is Pain – or Glory

I know many lonely people today who would like to have company. Families have grown and gone their way into the wide world. Some have trained in limited professions, and earned success, and that has enabled them to send from overseas good news of a rewarding kind. But they can seldom come back in person – and the years pass. Letters mean much, but never enough, for the home folks are left always to read between the lines.

On that far side of the world, new acquaintances and friends win a place in the pattern of the years, and the fullness of such relationships – even when they mean marriage and the founding of a new family – cannot be fully appreciated. Distance stretches between, and loneliness becomes something that must be handled secretly by the ageing father, the ageing mother. Courageously, even! However proud they are that they have been given to each other in birth and family sharing, a time always comes when distance or death means that one is very much alone.

To others known to me, a wartime marriage has come to mean a like severance. A young member of the family is whisked off to serve his country overseas, just at the time when he should be seeking a partner. Counting himself wonderfully fortunate, he finds one during leave-time, in England, Scotland, Wales. An engagement results, and at the cessation of hostilities marriage is planned for.

The prospect of a new home, in a country of which she has heard so much, seems to the girl a great adventure. And it is – all this, and more – for a time. Then, against the strangeness of some things, and the loss of old friends and old ways of doing things, she finds she can't settle. Then loneliness moves in. It is a familiar story.

And there are experiences of loneliness, often kept secret, that many single people know just as painfully. Though not by any means all. Some of us are temperamentally suited to it and like to be alone, if not all the time, at least for a lot of it. But nobody looking on would ever count us lonely, it is handled so well. Many professional women find themselves belonging to this group. And what a blessing many of these gifted single women are, to their city or community. Having come several times to "the crossroads of choice" they are content to centre their life in a flat and some chosen service in their free time. Church youth groups would be the poorer, were it not so; and choirs, and musical, cultural or artistic societies. And how would the compassionate affairs of child care and social service go forward without such free time help?

And this is not to overlook many fine single men I have found offering service every bit as essential – though I might leave one of their male benefactors to speak up for them!

For both parties, on this issue of loneliness, Dr Paul Tillich speaks well. A widely known modern Christian leader and writer, he says: "Our language wisely senses our nature. It has created the word *'loneliness' to express the pain of being alone*; and *it has created the word 'solitude' for the glory of being alone*."

True! And many whom I have come to admire have discovered for themselves the great difference between these two words, knowing both. One who greatly enriched my life was Richard Church, who for twenty-five years followed the family tradition of an English Civil Servant, resigning as soon as he was able to live by his pen. And countless of us readers the world around give thanks for that! The presence of a number of his refreshing books of essays and poems, on my handiest shelves, speaks for me; as does the place several letters over his signature hold, among others I have from writers, in a generous, fattening bundle. When I was engaged in writing my first anthology, at "West Hills", *Delight Upon Delight*, no one could have been more interested. Under themes that made up the framework of my undertakings, he allowed me the use of several of his poems; and again, several more when I was doing a follow-up, *People are People*. This is not to forget how often I have borrowed from my nearby library his admirable volume on the County of Kent, that I have come to know too, walking through it several times with my trusty haversack. It was a happy day that brought to Richard Church the opportunity to make his home there, on the edge of flowering orchards, in a transformed oast house. (But I should say, *their* oast house, since it was shared by his loved wife, a craftswoman and amateur architect.) At that time, he wrote a poem beginning:

> She sits beside our hearth,
> The girl I wooed so long
> With ardour and despair.
> Time has touched her gently,
> Put silver in her hair . . .

During the time I speak of, he was never "alone" in the painful sense of the word, though he knew well enough what it meant, before they met.

But he wrote beautifully, in its second sense, under the chosen chapter title of "Being Alone". "I am a man living in *solitude*", are his opening words. "That is living richly nowadays, for solitude becomes an increasingly expensive commodity in this shrinking world. I imagine that in a century to come it will be obtainable only by multi-millionaires, or super-commissars, or whatever the equivalent of the privileged few may be in that future dispensation. But at whatever price, *solitude remains, and will remain, the greatest jewel in the crown of human happenings*." There, in words that might seem to some poetical or even extravagant, is his evaluation of solitude, blessing him with creative quietness; birdsong heard through his study window with the beginning of each busy day, until its close, a pile of work behind him, he walks out alone under the sky over a nearby lane, his two cats following his footsteps in ready agreement. So bedtime finds him.

*

But others of us have to seek solitude in quite a different setting. I think of the widely revered Dag Hammarskjöld, who, until his tragic air crash on a mission of mercy, was Secretary-General of the United Nations. Some spoke of him as "a lonely man", but others, more fittingly, as "a solitary – one who had the wilderness for a pillow, and called the star his brother". And a beautiful secret there was in that! That supportive solitude gave him strength for living.

*

So it was in the experience of our Lord and Master, when here on earth. We read in the Gospels of an occasion, the crowds milling around Him, when "there was not time, even so much as to eat". No one got more into His days; needy crowds gathered, and milled about Him, wherever He went. In villages, on open spaces, even in houses where He entered, as Dr Luke records of one typical occasion (4:38–42; R.S.V.): "And He arose, and left the synagogue" – try to visualize it – "and entered Simon's house. Now Simon's mother-in-law was ill with a high fever, and they besought Him for her. And He stood over her, and rebuked the fever, and it left her; and immediately she rose and served them." (Just the kind of demand made upon Him that Luke, as a doctor, understood, and liked to report when he came to write his Gospel. But with time for no more than a breath, he goes on.) "Now when the sun was setting, all those who had any that were sick with various diseases brought them to Him; and He laid His

hands on every one of them and healed them. And demons
also came out of many, crying, You are the Son of God!
But he rebuked them and would not allow them to speak,
because they knew that He was the Christ." (And on we
go, to hear about the early beginning of another day.)
"And when it was day He departed and went into a lonely
place." (And well He needed to. But there is to be for Him
no solitude, even there; for Luke's Gospel goes on:) "And
the people sought Him and came to Him, and would have
kept Him from leaving them, but He said to them, I must
preach the good news of the Kingdom of God to the other
cities also . . ." (His God-given programme was in no sense
a limited, pleasant, easy undertaking – not at all. And time
in which to accomplish it would all too soon run out!)
"While the people pressed upon Him to hear the word of
God, He was standing by the Lake of Gennesaret; and He
saw two boats by the Lake; but the fishermen had gone out
of them, and were washing their nets. Getting into one of
the boats, which was Simon's." (Here He was with friends;
perhaps they could help Him to much-needed solitude, but
it was not easy. He stepped into the boat beached by
Simon.) "He asked him to put out a little from the land.
And He sat down and taught the people from the boat"
(Luke 5:1–3; R.S.V.). (There was a breath of fresh air
about Him now, and a little room to move, but not for long.
Soon we are reading:) "While He was in one of the cities,
there came a man full of leprosy; and when he saw Jesus,
he fell on his face and besought Him, Lord, if You will,
You can make me clean. And He stretched out His hand
. . ." (vv. 12, 13–16). "But so much the more the report
went abroad concerning Him; and great multitudes
gathered to hear and to be healed of their infirmities. *But
He withdrew to the wilderness and prayed.*"

*

And this is the essential secret in this chapter for us to
ponder; if our Lord couldn't manage without solitude in

His busy life – neither can we! Sometimes, it seems to us as hard to achieve as He found it. But find it we must, for we cannot live fully without it.

> There are burdens we can share with none,
> Save God.
> And paths remote where we must walk alone,
> With God.
> For lonely burdens, and for paths apart –
> Thank God!
> If these but serve to bring the burdened heart
> To God.

(Oxenham)

There is no need for you to tell me how you achieve this, nor for me to tell you how I do. One of the most ingenious ways was that favoured by that fine Christian, Dr Edward Wilson, who went South with Scott and has been a hero of mine ever since. In writing to his wife, he told of his search for solitude; but it was his mate, Cherry Garrard, in his Introduction to Wilson's biography, who first told his secret to the world. Against the background of the little, loaded ship that took them down to a task outside civilization, he wrote: "Courage, or ambition, or love of notoriety, may take you to the Antarctic, or any other uncomfortable place in the world, but it won't take you far inside without being found out; it's courage: and unselfishness: and helping one another: and sound condition: and willingness to put in every ounce you have: and clean living: and good temper: and good judgement: and faith . . . It has come almost as a shock to some of us", he had to write of Dr Edward Wilson, "to learn, for the first time, that he held a service to himself up in the crow's nest every week." There, in solitude, he nurtured his spirit, for the stubborn tests of life!

A Miracle to Match

I have known dear Edward and Lynn for many years, long
before they married. We used to belong to the same
discussion group, and that was fun. Since we've all left that
southern city and come north, we have seen a good deal of
each other.

Lynn phoned towards the end of last week to invite me
to Ed's birthday on Tuesday evening. "Just a small group,"
she said, "we haven't room in our flat for many – you'll
know them all. Most belong to the church, all about our
age."

And looking back now on Tuesday, I think what a
delightful evening it was. But one thing stands out: Ed
wouldn't say how old he was. I always imagined that this
was only an important secret to a woman, when a few silver
hairs began to show. But apparently not! His age, I imagine
on reflection, could have something to do with the job he
holds.

Age seems to some an important thing. My big *World
Language Dictionary* gave me the word in six languages,
besides our own English: French, German, Italian,
Spanish, Swedish and Yiddish. But that didn't help me
much. And my thoughts flew to a drawer in my study and
a story there of another Edward: Edward Verral Lucas, the
English author and essayist, and widely known servant of
Punch. He died in 1938 but before that I had a letter from
him, giving me permission to re-tell his story. And here it
is, prompted by the coincidence that both of these Edwards
show a concern for age.

E. V. Lucas wrote many books of essays, and when I was
building up my study library, some found a welcome there.
But this story, with its chuckle, is not among them. "It may

not be generally known", said Lucas, about the time that I happened to be making my first visit to an editor in Bouverie Street, London, "that Bouverie Street, in which the *Punch* office is situated, is steep and narrow and one-way, and is rendered exceedingly dangerous by lorries delivering huge rolls of paper on the east side, and every kind of vehicle descending on the west side at considerable speed, often silently, so close to the pedestrian, descending too, that if absentmindedly he stepped into the gutter he would immediately have his leg shaved off. This, complicated by the presence of a fleet of 'Special Edition' cars, is the normal condition of our thoroughfare, which at the present moment has been made even more perilous by the demolition and reconstruction of our premises, also on the west side, so that, with the removal of debris or the arrival of building material, the pavement can often be impassable.

"It was so the other day as I was making my way towards the Embankment, in the company of another writer for this paper whose initials are a household word.

"At a certain point opposite the scene of activity we were stopped by a wheelbarrow of cement, on the handles of which a labourer was for the moment seated. On noticing my approach, however, he rose and pushed it aside with the invitation, 'Come on, daddy'.

"Now, as we advance in years and begin to make more and more use of the handmirror with which to reflect the top of our heads, there are three ways in which we can behave. Although probably, underneath, resenting the process of age, we can affect indifference; we can pretend youthfulness, always hoping that by skilful combing and a general sprightly demeanour, the world is being taken in; or – and this is probably the least common attitude of the three – we can accept the situation and even go so far as to be older than we are.

"Which of them I, who am advancing in years, adopt, I do not intend to divulge, but I must confess that when I considered the courtesy with which the navvy made room for me to pass and heard his invitation, 'Come on, daddy', I was not too much pleased. Was it possible that I looked like that? Was the stigma of 'daddyness', or as he of course was thinking, 'grand-daddyness', all over me? I could not remember ever having been nailed in that way before – 'come on, daddy' – and frankly I was nettled. To be so patently and publicly a veteran!

"We had been talking quite gaily, the other and far more illustrious contributor and I, before the affair of the wheelbarrow intervened; and I seemed to have no more interest. Indeed, I might never have spoken again had he not remarked: 'That was a good one.'

"'What?' I asked coldly.

"'Why, calling you "laddy". Didn't you hear? He said, "Come on, laddy". I wish someone would call me that again.'

"'But he didn't', I replied. 'He said "daddy". Distinctly "daddy".'

"'Not a bit of it. He said "laddy".'

"'Sure?'

"'Absolutely. He said, "Come on, laddy". We'll go back and ask him if you're still doubtful.'

"'Oh, no', I said, already feeling more cheerful and again in tune with creation. 'If you're so convinced.'

"And I went on my way rejoicing.

"And thinking it over . . . Ah, well, we mustn't think these things over. Even if we cannot deceive ourselves, let us be grateful for them. 'Laddy'? Of course it was 'laddy'."

*

From the beginning, there is a special countenance belonging to each season of the year; so there is to every stage of one's ongoing life. And we like it that way. Childhood has its freshness, innocence, dependence; youth its conscious strength, eagerness and independence; and manhood or womanhood moves us each into a wider kingdom, with a new kind of pride. Though these "glories" are not so easily marked today. Once, a boy knew that he was moving up progressively, excitingly, satisfactorily, when he went into long pants – though usually only for Sunday, at the start. Then came his first job; his first pay envelope. And soon, his first sweetheart.

The way up for girls wasn't quite so clearly marked: only some went on to High School or College; some went to learn dressmaking or millinery, some went into what was called "service". I remember when the great moment came for me – when I could count myself a young woman, and go to business; and, what was more important, be so counted by other people. It was on a Sunday evening, the time we all went to the village Wesleyan Chapel, as a family, knowing everyone, and being known by everyone.

We had a visiting uncle to tea, and somehow he managed to set off the family discussion, on hearing that I was "going to work" on the morrow. They insisted that I should put up my hair. And what was more alarming – since I had a good healthy mop of it – they added the word "*Now!*" And there and then somebody volunteered to do my share of the drying up of the tea dishes, in the short time between the meal and leaving for church. Somebody else brought forth a mirror and a handful of hairpins. And hoping that they would all stay in place, we set off. It was only a matter of a few minutes' walk, but when we got there, our own pew was filled, and we had to go right to the very front – and with a head full of hairpins! Every eye in the Chapel focused interestedly in my direction. I don't remember in the least who the preacher was, whether our minister or a local preacher, or what the sermon was about. *To blush for a whole hour, is a bit of an undertaking*, and, where one was so well known, very painful!

Six years later, when the firm farewelled me with a speech, and a cup and saucer, I left to go south to train to be a long-time servant of the Church. And of my own will and desire, I sought out a beauty salon and, since it was now the fashion, had my hair cut – to be delivered from a lifelong servitude to hairpins. But I was now grown up!

*

The years, of course, can be greatly helped by an inheritance of good health; by having a place to live where one is wanted, and loved; by a life work that adds to the worthwhileness of the world, and the satisfaction of those who share it. But speaking for myself, I can't see that there is any reason ever to withhold the secret of one's age. Some, I know, refuse any reference to the approach of what we have been taught to call "middle age". Some fear it, though they never say why; or if they go secretly to discuss a critical birthday with a senior friend, or family doctor, keep it to themselves. And they have a right to, of course.

Since first I noticed dear Dr Luke's reference to it, in his Book of Acts, I have wonderingly underscored his words in my New Testament (4:22; A.V.). It concerns a man whom Peter and John, in their journey, happened on, *a man who needed a miracle in his life, as much as we all do for one reason or another*, as our birthdays roll by. He needed physical healing, which, of course, is not the only miracle God has in store for His children of men, through the gracious ministry of Christ.

But when the priests, and the captain of the Temple, and the Sadducees found themselves involved in this happening, they were upset. They didn't rightly know what to do, and being late in the day, they popped Peter and John into prison overnight, to give them time to think things out.

But it wasn't as easy as that (vv. 13–14): "Now when they saw the boldness of Peter and John," said Dr Luke, "and perceived that they were unlearned and ignorant men [or "untrained laymen", the New English Bible translates Dr Luke's words], they marvelled; and they took knowledge of them, that they had been with Jesus. And beholding the man which was healed standing with them, they could say nothing against it . . . [And now comes verse 22, that interests me so much at this moment, whilst we're thinking of birthdays, and the shyness of my two Edwards] *For the man was above forty years old, on whom this miracle was shewed.*"

Above forty years old – middle-aged, and more – Christ our Lord refuses to fix a date to a miracle. Aren't you glad about that? I am! Again and again, as we travel through this life, you and I need a miracle, to match our need!

And make no mistake – it will match our age!

In Quotation Marks

Sometimes, when a long-time reader of mine chances to meet me somewhere unexpectedly, he or she is in company, and I am introduced as "an author of many books". If there should be an awkward silence to bridge over, the stranger will take refuge in a question that's no longer new: "Which of all your books do you like the best?" A slight variation can be: "Which of your stories do you like the best?" (There's likely to be another pause after that – try asking a mother which of all her children she likes the best!)

I wonder whether anyone ever put such a question to Dr Luke? It's true that he only wrote two books: his Gospel and the Book of Acts, but within them he made a place for many stories. If he had to answer which of all he liked best, I wouldn't be surprised to hear him settle for the story of "The Thankful Leper" (Luke's Gospel, 17:11–19; A.V.). He wrote of Jesus, "It came to pass, as He went to Jerusalem, that He passed through the midst of Samaria and Galilee. And as He entered into a certain village, there met Him ten men that were lepers, which stood afar off: And they lifted up their voices, and said, 'Jesus, Master, have mercy on us.'

"And when He saw them, He said unto them, 'Go show yourselves unto the priests.'

"And it came to pass, as they went, they were cleansed.

"And one of them, when he saw that he was healed, turned back, and with a loud voice glorified God. And fell down on his face at His feet, *giving Him thanks*: and he was a Samaritan.

"And Jesus, answering said, 'Were there not ten cleansed? But where are the nine?'"

A great little human story it is, and an ageless one!

For thankfulness, of course, is an attitude of heart, rather than an occasional act, and I feel that Dr Luke must have found joy in the fact that this solitary thankful man was a stranger, a despised man, a Samaritan.

*

I am unprepared still to say which, of all the stories I have written over the years, is my favourite. A choice is not simple, and it is likely to vary – at one time it might be this one, at another, that.

But the story of an old friend, Tom Morland, that I wrote in an early book, *His Interpreters* (now out of print), is as fresh as ever, and may be unknown to many of my present-day readers. Besides that, it's closely linked with that story from Dr Luke. It runs:

I knew old Tom Morland well, from the time he began to tackle the class in the little country Sunday school. It wasn't a big class: there were only ten boys. If there had been more I don't know how old Tom would have managed. He was too gentle. No one in the whole valley was more surprised, of course, than the old man himself when he was asked to take them – they had no teacher, and unless somebody tried, they would have no class.

Those ten boys seemed to have more youthful devilry packed into them than most. The first morning, the old man faced them with the story of the ten lepers healed by Christ – a lesson that had cost him half a week of evenings in preparation. They began by asking if it was true.

Somehow the old man managed week after week to keep their interest. Ten years went by, and there are many Sundays in ten years.

He has gone now; he died last autumn. He got very frail towards the end, and had to leave the valley and live with his son up in town. The Silver Jubilee was held at the little valley church, but he couldn't go. The guest speaker for that occasion was a distinguished Christian doctor. He wasn't eloquent, but his being there at all was the most eloquent witness of the Jubilee. The whole burden of his brief talk was about a class of ten boys.

And how glad he must be now that he sat down and wrote a letter to one who was not there to hear his speech of thanks. For the Jubilee was scarcely over when there was a familiar name in the obituaries.

I saw that letter. Old Tom showed it to me with wonder in his pale blue eyes. "Bless the good Lord!" he kept saying, his frail old mind mixing things up a bit. "True? Didn't I say it was true – that there were ten of them, *and one of them came back to say his thanks!*"

*

"Bless the Lord, O my soul," cried the psalmist, from the deep-bubbling depths of his heart, "and forget not all His benefits" (Psalm 103:2; A.V.). Our ageless Communion Service says that "it is meet, right, and our bounden duty, that we should at all times, and in all places, give thanks unto Thee, O Lord . . ." But if we are thankful only because it is our duty, we have not fully entered into the joyous depths of this glorious experience called "Thanksgiving"! A modern-day writer, J. Neville Ward, in a fine chapter headed "Thanking" in one of his books, says: "Life, if it is lived thankfully, is well on the way to becoming a holy thing."

It may begin with a very simple action, as did that one valley boy in an old man's class of ten; or as G. K. Chesterton liked to tell of, out of his experience. In his early years, when he was not yet clear what to think or what to do with his life, he managed to come through a trying time. He tells us that he "*hung on to the remains of religion by one thin thread of thanks*".

And many another of us has laid hold of this secret early in life, and continued to embrace it through the years, not

because it is "meet, right, and our bounden duty" – but for
very joy and wonder! One says, from the deep places of his
heart:

> What do I owe?
> Yea, Lord, what do I not?
> All that I am –
> And all that I have got.
> (Anon)

I might have been very shy of Helen Keller when I was
privileged to meet her, had she not already sent me a
precious letter of thanks. It was handwritten, in her bold
open hand, each letter squared on the top and bottom, as
are those resulting from the use of a frame. She had visited
a fine Library for the Blind in the south of Australia, before
coming on to New Zealand, and had happened on a
number of my books there, made available in Braille, so
she had written to thank me, on her own account and on
behalf of those using the Library. She, better than anyone
the world round, was in a position to know what books
could mean to the blind, not only because she had been
blind nearly all her life; but because she was not only a
reader, but a writer too.

In her book *Midstream*, she had expressed her deep
thanks, and I had taken time to copy out her words.
"Perhaps it is true of everyone," she wrote, "but it seems
to me that in a special way, what I read becomes part of
me." She went on: "What I am conscious of borrowing
from my author friends, I put in quotation marks" – as we
all must, or find ourselves getting into great trouble with
the copyright laws that govern publications. (But, in any
case, the average author, greatly enriched by the efforts of
others, would want to express thanks.)

And then, she continued: "But I do not know how to
indicate the wandering seeds that drop unperceived into
my soul." Nor do I. I can only return, like the grateful leper

Dr Luke tells us of, to the Divine Giver of all good. Or, like the grown-up class boy – one of ten – in the experience of old Tom Morland, do the best I can, by way of a little speech, when a likely opportunity shows up. Helen Keller has her own way, as we each must. She continues: "I prefer to put quotation marks at the beginning and end of my book, and leave it to those who have contributed to its interest or charm or beauty to take what is theirs, and accept my gratitude for the help they have given to me."

And many of us feel that we should do that with our lives – if only it were possible to affix quotation marks at either end of a busy, happy, rich life! Few days have come and gone without some fresh awareness of truth and beauty, some lovely action witnessed in commonplace circumstances, some act of courage before the going down of the sun. Splendid books continue to be written and published, despite much paper wasted on rubbish. Many great thoughts are captured in poetry; many a burden lightened by the wings of song.

One of our contemporary authors, Storm Jameson, in writing her autobiography, finished as fittingly as any of us might, with a lengthy listing of experiences grim and gay, and the simple, unforgettable words: "*For what I have received, may the Lord make me truly thankful . . .!*"

One of Life's Great Words

The more I think of a brief saying of Sir Walter Raleigh, the more I find in it of lasting significance. "*Life*", he said, "*is spent in learning the meaning of great words.*"

Soldier, courtier, explorer, author – the whole dictionary lay open to him, as in a fuller degree today it lies open to us. "Courage" is there, and "kindness" and "courtesy", and all the rest now precious to us. But I feel sure Raleigh was not thinking of "great words" of the dictionary, but of the heart. And these don't change very much. "The only things that change radically in life", said H. V. Morton in our day, "are fashions and inventions. The human heart was patented long ago, and the Creator has not seen fit to bring out a later model."

I know what he means; for the "great word" that I find myself pondering at the moment, is the word *Home*. It belongs to the heart, wherever it is, not to the dictionary, nor even to building materials, routine bricks and mortar.

The simplest homes I have come upon are dry caves, on the western slopes of Mount Carmel, near Haifa, where men and women, not very different from us at heart, set up home thousands of years ago. And I have considered colourless camelhair tents, to this day spread out on the stony levels under the merciless sun near Jericho. And sun-baked mud bricks that serve as building materials for others that I have looked upon with interest in my travels – for I am a home lover.

I first learnt that long ago when, as a young child, I went to stay with some folk in the country. They were very welcoming. We did a lot of things – gathered mushrooms in the grass, and caught funny little things in the creek. But it wasn't a success – I got home-sick. And what a lovely place home seemed in that hour!

But that is one thing that holidays are for, somebody has tried to persuade me since – and he might well be right. We sit up to a strange table, where nobody has been taught to say "Grace", and it doesn't seem right; and day after day, meal after meal, what comes on our plates is different. And an ordinary boiled egg for tea, with toast fingers, seems wonderful – because it belongs to home; though many a time *there*, we had to be encouraged to "sit up and eat it up". For the first time we are taken to the beach, to sit on the sand; or we go to throw stones into a strange pond. But the lesser attractions of our little stream at the end of the cow paddock at home mean more to us. And it isn't only an experience of childhood – all our life through, though in a less painful way, we go off to the ends of the earth on holiday, by this time maybe mingled with business. But always it ends the same way – in that moment when we say: "*It's nice to be home!*" And it is. There's something special about home – and it isn't a matter of architecture.

We've come a long way since childhood, with wood, stone and plaster, completely insulated – damp-proof, rot-proof and sound-proof, whether near the kindly earth or high into the sky. The very latest homes, I am told, are of plastic, as belonging to the space age. Each has a transparent roof, and walls to trap sunshine, and through all the hours of the day give diffused lighting. Permanent colour characterizes such a house, I am told, so that there will never be any need to redecorate. But wouldn't that be a little dull? One possible change so far promised, is that one could take one's plastic building apart, and set it up in a new place. (But this is but a building I'm talking about, and important as it might be that's not a home. A home is much more than materials. The little child of refugee parents was near a deep spiritual truth when, on being asked whether they had a home, said: "Yes, we have a home – but no house to put around it.")

A good, sound building, happily set and weather-proof,

is important; and it's hard to build a home without such essentials. Yet countless families in our world today do lack them.

The earliest houses raised by colonists in New Zealand – where a home awaited me when I was born – were simple in some respects. Most were built of wood, soundly and well – but they did not lack love. And that is what makes a house a *home*! Ours was of that kind.

And in maturity – long after I had left home for the wider world, I am thankful to say – I was in time to be received by Miss Gertrude Matilda Kemp in *the oldest wooden house in New Zealand*. (The house itself is still there, standing two-storeyed in the position it has always occupied, in the far North. But Miss Kemp is no longer there.) I shall never forget that sunny, blue-sky afternoon, and the simple, old-fashioned flowers in the garden as I approached the front door, many in sweet, full bloom, blessed by visiting bees. It was not just an historic house – it was a Home, and had been from the start, for a missionary family lived there. Everybody far and near in the Bay of Islands knew the Kemps, an early Anglican missionary family.

Miss Kemp took me, at a leisurely pace, from room to room. She had many good pioneer stories to tell; during her eighty-one years, she had lived in no other house.

And on Sundays she loved to go up to the little church on the hill nearby, to worship with others from Keri-keri, and to play the organ.

But no homely story that I heard that day is more dear to me than that of her own good, faithful spirit. (I asked her to tell it to me as someone had long ago told me of her lamp, before ever that opportunity had come to go north and visit the old house, "the old home".)

Nearby, in the front where we looked out, was a tidal waterway, and as long as life was hers, my old hostess kept a lighted lamp in the front window after dark, to guide any little ships that might come up the inlet.

Ever since – thinking over my visit – it has seemed to me that that lively, loving care was of the true spirit of Home, wherever, and however, it might be expressed.

About the time of my visit, Evelyn Underhill – one of the sensitive Christian writers whose books we welcomed – was reminding us that when God sent His Son Jesus into our world, it was into a modest home in Nazareth. So important did He think a home to be! And it was but a carpenter's home, not even that of a priest. There God knew, that – with Mary, a young village maiden become his wife and the Babe's mother – was provided all that was needed. "We see the new life", said Evelyn Underhill, "growing in secret. Nothing very startling happens. We see the child in the carpenter's shop. He does not go outside the frame of the homely life in which He appeared. It did quite well for Him, and will do quite well for us . . . for the pressure of God's Spirit is present everywhere . . . Our environment itself, our home and our job is the medium through which we experience the moulding of His besetting love."

That puts it well! And it is a thousand pities that in our midst today are many who do not acknowledge this. Many home relationships have broken up, in one way and another, with home love and family security lost. The divorce rate has grown to colossal proportions. "Home", for many, is no longer one of life's big words as it was when Dr Luke wrote (Luke 4:16–22; A.V.).

The sacred stability of home was in jeopardy before ever war came – that gets blamed for a good deal, and it is true that hurried war engagements and war weddings were, of necessity, a feature of those times. More distressing still was the great number of relationships that did not wait on a leave-time engagement or wedding.

As far back as the year 1858, we are told, the annual divorce rate in Britain was twenty-four. By 1920 (that's the end of the First World War) it had grown to three thousand; and those who knew about it, or were in any way affected tried to hush it up. By 1944, it had grown to nineteen thousand, and it was hopeless to try to hush it up. In long-drawn-out war years – when our kinsfolk, sons and daughters from all over the world, were battling for military victory – the battle in many parts was being lost on the home front; and I use the words in their closest, unchanging, supportive sense. During that same time, some thirty-three thousand illegitimate children were born in Britain alone. Many of them, by now in middle age, have I no doubt grown up well enough – but something has been lost.

I can't think of anyone – apart from Christ his Master – more welcome to cross doorsteps than Dr Luke. Doctors have always embraced this special privilege, and it's a matter of much more than pills and potions. Studdert-Kennedy – as we all may know – was not a doctor, but a wholly devoted servant of Christ, a clergyman who, in our troubled century, when so many good values have been torn apart, said: *"The primary school of vital and vitalizing Love is the Home!"*

Lest We Give Ourselves Away

Our young people became excited at the prospect of the Annual Youth Party, a fancy dress occasion, and as the night drew near, I began to think about my own costume. A few years before I had seen a jovial representation of the Michelin Tyre man, worn in a students' University Rag, and I wondered whether it would do. At the first opportunity, I sought out the city office of the tyre agent, and quickly came to the point: "Could I hire the outfit for a young people's party?" "Certainly, Madam." "I suppose I could get into it?" "Surely, Madam." "And what fee do you charge?" "Oh," came the unexpected answer, "it's free! Just give us your name and address, and the date, and we'll see that you get it."

I came out on to the street again, jubilant. But a week later, when I arrived home for tea on the date of the party, it hadn't come.

Then presently, a lorry backed in, and a man knocked at our door. "Where do you want this thing?" he asked, with a sweep of his hand towards his load, a packing case about the size of a piano. "Round the back," I answered blithely. "Have you a man about the place who could help me?" was his next enquiry. Then my friend Rene set on to me: "To think you're going to a party", she said, "in a thing that a man can't lift!" However, when I'd wrenched off the lid, it wasn't quite as bad as that – the timber of the case was an inch thick.

Then came the business of getting into the "rig". In three parts it was: the legs in the likeness of a series of small tyres, it went on like a pair of pants with braces. Next came the body – a large arrangement of tyres, also of canvas whitened over. Then the head piece. To the weighty, suffo-

145

cating whole I added heavily rimmed glasses, and to my feet, a pair of black leather slippers. At that moment, I decided that I must never speak a word the whole evening. I had already taken off my watch and ring, in case anyone recognized them. Next, I sent a note to the leader of the party, very carefully worded, saying that I was sorry that they wouldn't *see me* at the party, after all.

And just on starting-time at eight, having begged the use of a neighbour's front bedroom to get into my "rig", I bounced my way in among the youngsters. For the next hour or two that got hotter and hotter, I was at their mercy, and I can't ever remember a party where I worked so hard. The leader, taking his place in the middle of things, read out my note to accompanying groans and sighs, and from the parents immediate speculation as to what illness could have overwhelmed me.

Believe it or not, I actually managed to keep silent for two hours, but even added to my care over the watch and ring, that wasn't enough. I'd forgotten about my double-jointed thumb. From the far end of the hall came a cry that brought us all to a standstill: "I know who it is – *look at her thumb*!"

I'd given myself away! And several of those youngsters, grown up now, have never let me forget it.

Of course, this is more than party fun! My thoughts go back to Peter, disciple of our Master, and what Dr Luke wrote of him when Jesus was standing trial. It was a chilly night; and Peter was drawn to pass the time beside a fire of coals that had been lit "in the midst of the hall" (Luke 22:55–62). "And a certain maid beheld him as he sat by the fire . . . and said, This man was also with Him. And he denied any knowledge of Him. And after a little while another saw him, and said: Thou art also of them. And Peter said, Man, I am not. And about the space of an hour after, another confidently affirmed, saying, Of a truth, this fellow also was with Him; for he is a Galilean." Or as Matthew records this third charge, as the firelight flickers across Peter's face: "*Thy speech betrayeth thee.*" It did! Peter, unthinkingly, "gave himself away". As scholars remind us, in *The Interpreter's Bible*, "Peter's accent was Galilean. The Aramaic of Galilee, like the Arabic spoken there today, had dialectical peculiarities."

*

It is not a matter of *accent* with us, as servants of the same Christ. It's our common, everyday behaviour, our standard of values in the home, in the office, the shop, the hospital, on the tennis court. Observers are very shrewd. They can tell whether our Christian discipleship is real, or not. If there is any question about our relationship with our Lord it will soon be known – we give ourselves away, all too easily.

And in lots of other ways, we unthinkingly show our values – even the keeping of an ordinary diary will do that. Most of us keep our diaries secret, but more than likely there will come a day when other eyes will scrutinize what *we* have written. It was so with the father of Edmund Gosse, and his son held it against him for a lifetime. You may have read the widely known book Sir Edmund Gosse wrote, *Father and Son*, telling of these things. The father, Philip Henry Gosse, was a naturalist. For nine years of his career he played an important role in the British Museum, in London. His being a naturalist contributed, maybe, to the values at his life's centre – I don't know. But not wholly; I feel in no sense called to make excuses for him. Values are values! It's true that he didn't marry till late in life – a good woman at his side early in life would surely have made a difference. We don't know. It was also true that the woman he eventually did marry was no longer young. They were neither of them much used to children, and there is some doubt whether they ever entertained any expectation of having a child of their own.

But the day came when their only son, Edmund, was born. And it was the entry in his father's diary for that day, which left him all his life long with an unhappy sense of being poorly received. It gave him away! That entry read, under the birth date: "E. delivered of a son. Received green swallow from Jamaica." That's all. But doesn't it say a lot about values? There is no fatherly spirit, no family rejoicing – a boy and a bird are made to seem of about the same importance!

But a boy is an eternal spirit whereas a bird is not, for all that God makes both of them, and gives them to live in His world. Philip Henry Gosse is sadly wanting in everyday Christian values. We are not judging him – he gives himself away!

"Jesus Christ", said Harnack, the great Christian scholar to whom we owe so much, "was the first to bring *the value of every human soul* to light." There is no story in the New Testament showing Jesus, under any circumstances, undervaluing a human being. Our word "respect", we are told, comes from a Latin word meaning "to look again". Jesus was always doing that – never satisfied with a snap evaluation. Had that been His approach, Peter the fisherman, in his scaly, smelly fishing clothes, could never have been chosen as one of the Twelve. Nor could the sound of his impetuous voice, above the heads of his work mates, have suggested a successful preacher of the eternal love of God. Peter, to our Lord, was a person – someone to be respected for who he was as well as for what he might become. And history proves how well worth "a second look" he was. To our Lord, everyone with breath in his lungs, and gifts of personality given by God, *was someone*. Even a poor, wretched robber, strung up on a cross within hailing distance of Him, was worth considering a candidate for Paradise!

Beside these, there was Zacchaeus, Matthew, Mary Magdalene and many another in Dr Luke's Gospel, who were never before properly valued till the Giver of life came by – and for them life ever afterwards became a different thing. His ministry and message were built around *lasting spiritual values*. He talked with children and gathered them in His arms; He lived among people "on the bread line" – craftsmen, housewives, shepherds, men waiting in the marketplace, who knew what it was like to have no work. He felt for the host who, in an emergency, had to wake up a kindly neighbour if he was to have bread to put before a hungry friend who had come on a journey. He knew, not only that people of all ages had clamant material needs, but *needed above all to be valued*.

And that is His message which comes down to us each very strongly, in contrast to father Gosse's diary entry, although some, even in our day, don't seem to have caught its secret. Their behaviour, when they are not aware of being watched, "gives them away".

David Blackhall, the blind poet of our day, tells of his early childhood in a large family. "At mealtimes", he began, "we would all be waiting at the table for Father. Mother would be standing in the window, looking across to the workshop. We fidgeted and whispered and eyed the food and waited for the word.

"'Quiet, everybody!' Mother would say briskly, beginning to bustle. 'Here comes your father.'

"When Father sat down at the table we could all start. Two rounds of bread and butter was the ration for tea, and, if you were lucky and it was your turn, the top of Father's boiled egg. A golden day in every sense was when Father cut deep and there was a fragment of yolk left in the top.

"By the time Don left school we all had bicycles and we were bringing a little money home. Mrs Stamford, who lived a few doors away, must have thought five sons a very considerable number. She had one son to her name, and he kept badgering her for a bicycle.

"'Certainly not', she said firmly. 'I should be worried to death every time you went out.'

"'But Mother', pleaded young Stamford, 'all Mrs Blackhall's boys have bicycles.'

"'I have only one son', she explained patiently, 'Mrs Blackhall has five. *She wouldn't miss one.*' Mrs Stamford herself recounted this episode to my mother . . . Mother was amused to think that anyone could imagine that if *one* of them didn't come home, it wouldn't be noticed."

Togetherness

What are your favourite words? Most of us do have favourites; and it's good to keep them in the forefront of thought.

I forget exactly how many words we are supposed to use every day, in our comings and goings, but it must be thousands. Experts have worked it out. I should think it would depend on whether we are naturally quiet folk; whether we live and work in isolation, or in the pressing city bustle of the crowd. And the nature of our occupation must make a difference too – teachers, preachers, politicians, auctioneers, broadcasters multiply words continually, whereas others of us are a little uneasy when speech is called for.

An early favourite word of mine was "Togetherness". I don't know now where I picked it up, but for a long time, I was a little shy about using it, when I failed to find it in the Oxford Dictionary. "Perhaps", I found myself saying under my breath, "it isn't a real word."

By the time I'd reached my middle thirties, in writing a book of devotions called *While the Candle Burns*, I boldly set the word "Togetherness" as the title of my first chapter. "Friendship spells 'Togetherness'", I wrote there – "one of the most beautiful things in the world, just 'Togetherness'". And I got a photographic artist to pose for me a striking picture of two young people coming up a hill together, hands linked, the girl a little ahead of the boy and setting the pace. There were clouds, but there was light above and the light was in their faces. I quoted Principal Rainy: "Through work and play alike, they dream of the great and happy future, and the part they too will play . . . Eternity is in their dreams." That's a long time ago now, but I still turn with refreshment to that page on "Togetherness" and the study following. There, I find myself quoting Tennyson's words – and they are fine words that never die, never age:

> The woman's cause is man's; they rise or sink
> Together, dwarfed or godlike, bond or free:
> If she be small, slight-natured, miserable,
> How shall men grow?

And one day, I chanced to discover that the word "Togetherness" had got into the dictionary. The entry in my new *Britannica World Language Dictionary* was brief – but it was there as : *The state of being associated or united.* It wasn't much to say about one of life's most beautiful realities, but perhaps it's enough – life is not long enough to express its full beauty and wonder.

That may well be the reason why God gives us the promise of life beyond this human earth experience that we know for a handful of years, and then must surrender.

It's not very often that one comes across a casual person who chances in the course of conversation to say, "I'm not really interested. I don't care whether Death is the end or not. 'Togetherness' means nothing to me." When it does happen, I find myself saying – if only under my breath – with Dr John Baillie: "Surely, in no mood can I contemplate the death of the most precious person I know . . . and say 'I do not care whether that is the end or not' . . . The man who can see his beloved die, believing that it is for ever, and say, 'I don't care', is a traitor to his beloved, and to all that love has brought. *He has no right not to care*." I think of my dear friend Rene.

Most of us do care greatly about the ending of an experience of "Togetherness" here, and the assurance that it will continue, in God's good planning, beyond this life. Here He gives us, we believe, much that can never die, and "Togetherness" is central to that gift.

I like very much the way Dean Matthews puts it: "Belief in God, means that the world is justified because it produces values . . . Whenever you speak of truth, goodness, and beauty, *you have in mind persons . . .* Truth which is not known is not truth, goodness which is not willed is not goodness, and beauty which is not enjoyed is not beauty . . . If God created, and sustains the universe, we are bound to believe that He created it for the sake of the good which it might contain, and that the good is reflected in persons, when they have become, as it were, a part of the good for which the world exists. He preserves them as part of that growing treasure which is the harvest of Time.

"Thus, we are emboldened to believe that persons, who seem to the superficial view so much less permanent than the mountains or even their own buildings, *are the most enduring of all created things.*"

I am copying this, I need hardly add, not as a piece of neat prose, but as a piece of living experience closely supporting; since it is yet but so short a time since the accident and death of my dearest friend, Rene, ending an earth-togetherness of fifty-two years.

*

But for togetherness of this kind to be real at the end of the way, I must say that it must be real all along the way. It is something welded of greater and lesser experiences. It is not a matter just of proximity – far from it – for it can be real with the material distance of a world between. My friend and I early discovered that. We shared a first world journey of a year together – and it was a wonderful experience; and we shared a second one much, much later. But in between, in the course of my writing-lecturing undertakings, I several times circled this same earth on my own, making many strange stops. I can't say that there were not times when I thought longingly of home, times when I got tired, travelling by ship, plane, and varied surface means of transport; or times when my obligations were almost too demanding.

But our long-experienced sense of togetherness held, and was to me beautifully, joyfully strong! The truth is, it was no casual thing. Letters to and fro were not only the proof of that – though proof they were – one awaiting me, together with my business correspondence, at every fresh home or hotel known to be taking me in. To achieve that, of course, much time and careful planning was necessary in Rene's busy teaching career, so far away, if mails were to connect and arrive on time. But it was the spirit of the undertaking that most gloriously spelled "Togetherness", as simply and beautifully we understood it, expressed by a favourite quotation we had long treasured. It said: "Those children of God to whom it has been given to see each other face to face, and to hold communion together, and to feel the same spirit working in both, can never more be sundered, though the hills may lie between. For their souls are enlarged for ever more by that union, and they bear one another about in their thoughts continually, as it were a new strength."

It was never, we knew, necessary to be together in one place to know this rich experience of "Togetherness". (One could sit together with another at a meal, yet in reality be actually miles apart in spirit. One could walk at another's side through a piece of countryside, and never once step over the threshold of his mind.)

Away back in Eden, when the newly created world was unpeopled, God saw an essential of its long adventure in terms of "Togetherness", and of the first man, said: "It is not good that he should live alone!" And forthwith God, in His graciousness, set about providing for that need, and so continues, in one way or another, until this day. For some, it is all wrapped up in terms of family life, so that often the brightest pages of history through the centuries have been those that have borne the names of "James Smith *and wife*". And Aquila *and* Priscilla are known for hospitality in the early hard days of the Church, which Dr Luke reported in his Book of the Acts. In chapter 18, verse 2 he introduces them and in missionary endeavour of like heroic proportions, as the years have rolled towards our time no two names shine with greater lustre than those of Adoniram Judson, *and his valiant wife Ann*, serving in Burma. And closer still in place and time, God's glorious ministry, expressed through "Togetherness", came to many in our day through Canon Barnett *and his wife*, whose two lives burned "as a single flaming candle" in the darkness of London's East End.

Good – or Grim?

I have long wondered why this day should be called "Good Friday", and very likely you have, too, since it was the day on which our Lord, a young man, was crucified, on the Hill of Crosses Three. It seems that it should more fittingly have been called "Grim Friday", but somehow it never has been.

The Gospels – every one of them, including that given us by Dr Luke – underline as graphically as words can do, the dastardly deed done that day (Luke 22:39–53; A.V.). And no words of mine can better those with which Luke's story comes to us, with a shock, in translation; all the more so because Judas, one of His Twelve, had a hand in it, with a night arrest by flickering torch light, in the retreat of Gethsemane's olive garden. That job done, the soldiers handed Him over to the authorities, accompanied by lashings, and the poor semblance of a trial, added to by cries from the screaming crowds: "Crucify Him! Crucify Him!"

Jesus was pushed from one point to another through the hours of night. The sleepy city, soon waking from its own affairs, joined those already assembled in the narrow street, winding and climbing out beyond the city wall. The prisoner was required to carry His own cross, until the weight of it, following the heavy happenings of the night, bore Him down. Then, as the custom was – since Palestine was an occupied country, and any man could be immediately impressed for service to the Roman authorities – a tap on the shoulder with the flat blade of a spear brought a dark-skinned stranger to an unexpected task. "Simon the Cyrenian", on a journey from far-off Cyrene (now known as Tripoli to many of our soldiers), found himself bearing a cross. Of the actual situation he knew little or nothing; but his service that day made him immortal. Luke is moved to name him in his Gospel (23:26; A.V.). And a Negro writer near our own time (Countee Cullen, 1903–46), feeling that he understood how Simon felt about things, wrote a poem to speak for him:

> He never spoke a word to me,
> And yet He called my name;
> He never gave a sign to me,
> And yet I knew and came.
>
> At first I said, "I will not bear
> His cross upon my back;
> He only seeks to lay it there
> Because my skin is black."
>
> But He was dying for a dream,
> And He was very meek,
> And in His eyes there shone a gleam
> Men journey far to seek.
>
> It was Himself my pity bought;
> I did for Christ alone
> What all of Rome could not have wrought
> With bruise of lash or stone.

Immediately after telling of Simon's part that day, in the journey that led the Saviour through the streets to His Crucifixion, by way of the Via Dolorosa, Dr Luke, with great feeling, mentions "two others with Him, criminals who were being led away to crucifixion; and when they reached the place called The Skull, they crucified Him there, and the criminals with Him, one on His right and the other on His left. Jesus said: 'Father, forgive them; they do not know what they are doing.'" And that prayer for those who, by their contrived judgement, had brought Him to that place, and which is recorded in Luke's Gospel (chapter 23, verse 34; the New English Bible), is never to be forgotten.

The chapter goes on to tell of the remaining events of that day: "His friends had all been standing at a distance; the women who had accompanied Him from Galilee stood with them and watched it all.

"Now there was a man called Joseph, a member of the Council, a good, upright man, who had dissented from their policy and the action they had taken. He came from the Judaean town of Arimathaea, and he was one who looked forward to the Kingdom of God. This man now approached Pilate, and asked for the body of Jesus. Taking it down from the cross, he wrapped it in a linen sheet," Luke says very reverently, "and laid it in a tomb cut out of the rock, in which no one had been laid before. It was Friday, and the Sabbath was about to begin." As verse 54, says in the A.V: "That day was the preparation, and the Sabbath drew on". But to say: "*It was Friday*", as the New English Bible does, introduces a shock of reality that must be considered.

For I was in Jerusalem one Friday, a while ago, and walked with a little gentle group of Franciscans, who led a modern-day procession from point to point of the Via Dolorosa. Anyone who is ready to join quietly, prayerfully with others of like spirit, might still tread that sorrowful way, in remembrance. I shall never forget it; it comes to my mind, every time I read my New English Bible: "*It was Friday.*"

But still it was not called "*Good* Friday". That, scholars tell me, didn't come till long afterwards. "And how, and why?" I want to ask, as you may, too. So I spent time going back to the records, for as far back as we have them. They were all rather vague; but in general they agreed upon one thing: "The term 'Good Friday' is counted to be a corruption of 'God's Friday'. It was called 'Long Friday' by the Anglo-Saxons and Danes", my *Encyclopedia*

Britannica, the best record I have, tells me – probably because of the long service of remembrance marking the day. Of one thing only can we be sure: among those involved in the loss of their dear Master at the time, nothing in that Friday could be called "Good", when that day came to an end. A lover of the Crucified, looking back reverently but imaginatively to that day's grimness, said:

> I heard two soldiers talking
> As they came down the hill –
> The sombre hill of Calvary,
> Bleak and black and still.
> And one said: "The night is late;
> These thieves take long to die."
> And one said, "I am sore afraid,
> And yet I know not why."
>
> I heard two women weeping
> As down the hill they came,
> And one was like a broken rose,
> And one was like a flame.
> One said, "Men shall rue
> This deed their hands have done."
> And one said only through her tears,
> "*My Son! My Son! My Son!*"

> (Unknown poet)

*

We ordinary Christian people, on this side of that grim event, cannot easily assign to it the name "Good Friday". "The origin of a yearly commemoration of the Crucifixion is somewhat obscure", says *The Encyclopedia Britannica*. "It may be regarded as certain that among Jewish Christians, it almost imperceptibly grew out of the old habit of annually celebrating the Passover, on the 14th of Nisan, and of observing the 'days of unleavened bread' from the 15th to the 21st of that month. In the Gentile churches, on the other hand, it seems to be well established that originally no yearly cycle of festivals was known at all.

"From its earliest observance, the day was marked by a specially rigorous fast; and also, on the whole, by a tendency to greater simplicity in the services of the Church. Prior to the fourth century, there is no evidence of non-celebration of the eucharist on Good Friday; but after that date the prohibition of communion became common. In Spain, indeed, it became customary to close the churches altogether as a sign of mourning . . . In the Roman Catholic Church the Good Friday ritual at present observed is marked by many special features, most of which can be traced back to a date at least prior to the close of the eighth century. In the Anglican Church, the observance of the day is more marked than formerly with meditation and silent prayer." Solemn Good Friday hymns usually have an important place, along with readings from the Gospels and penitential prayers, in most of the world Methodist and Presbyterian congregations that I know. During the last few years, Good Friday morning services have, in many places I know, found a helpful celebration through the use of symbols – the Towel; the Bread and Wine; central of all, the Cross, with its crown of thorns.

Even if there is no established historic reason for the name "Good" Friday, perhaps it is deemed above all things in the Faith, "Good" that *on the Cross Christ's Death – joined to His so-soon Resurrection of Easter Day – could only be joined as one in triumph, and counted good . . .!*

At the Very Heart of Things

The sun had not yet risen when, with two friends, I set out from the heart of Athens. Very few besides ourselves were yet on the streets, but despite the strangeness of it all, we stepped out confidently. The old door-keeper had given us clear directions, and even accompanied us a short distance on our way.

The tall Parthenon, standing pale against the morning sky, set our hearts beating with expectation, and soon we found ourselves ascending the ancient rocky face that, without doubt, had changed little over the years. In a short time we were actually standing on Mars' Hill, familiar to us through Dr Luke's "Acts of the Apostles". As the day opened out, crowds assembled in the place that – in Paul's day and before – had always been a place of crowds. But no visiting speakers engaged in public utterance were there, as once would have been the case. Modern scientists tell us that every sound, every statement uttered by the human voice, still lingers in the air, although we may not be sensitive enough to pick it up. This has always seemed incredible to me, and at no time more so than when we stood that morning on Mars' Hill. Though we were unable to hear the echo of Paul's voice itself, part of his famous speech that was familiar in our New Testament (Acts 17:16–34) was set there in bronze to speak to us through the centuries, in exquisitely lettered Greek. Dr Luke had succeeded in reporting Paul, as he began to speak with disarming courtesy on that far-away occasion, to those Athenian lovers of religious and philosophical argument: "Now while Paul waited . . . at Athens, his spirit was stirred in him, when he saw the city wholly given to idolatry. Therefore disputed he in the synagogue with the Jews, and

G.C.–F

161

with the devout persons, and in the market daily with them
that met with him.

"Then certain philosophers of the Epicureans, and of the
Stoicks, encountered him. And some said, What will this
babbler say? other some, He seemeth to be a setter forth
of strange gods: because he preached unto them *Jesus and
the resurrection*. And they took him, and brought him unto
Areopagus, saying, May we know what this new doctrine,
whereof thou speakest, is? For thou bringest certain
strange things to our ears: we would know therefore what
these things mean. (For all the Athenians and strangers
which were there spent their time in nothing else, but either
to tell, or to hear some new thing.)

"Then Paul stood in the midst of Mars' Hill, and said,
Ye men of Athens, I perceive that in all things ye are too
superstitious. For as I passed by, and beheld your
devotions, I found an altar with this inscription, TO THE
UNKNOWN GOD. Whom therefore ye ignorantly
worship, Him declare I unto you. God that made the world
and all things therein, seeing that He is Lord of heaven and
earth, dwelleth not in temples made with hands; neither is
worshipped with men's hands, as though He needed any
thing, seeing He giveth to all life, and breath, and all
things; and hath made of one blood all nations of men for
to dwell on all the face of the earth, and hath determined
the times before appointed, and the bounds of their
habitation; that they should seek the Lord, if haply they
might feel after Him, and find Him, though He be not far
from every one of us: for in Him we live, and move, and
have our being; as certain also of your own poets have said,
For we are also His offspring. Forasmuch then as we are
the offspring of God, we ought not to think that the
Godhead is like unto gold, or silver, or stone, graven by art
and man's device . . .

"And when they heard of the resurrection of the dead,
some mocked: and others said, We will hear thee again of
this matter. So Paul departed from among them. Howbeit

certain men clave unto him, and believed." And with that division of his hearers into three ageless groups, the record from Luke's pen comes to a close, but so graphic it is that we need little imagination to see that crowd – especially if it has been our privilege really to do so, as it was that morning mine!

Luke leaves us in no doubt that it was on the glorious message of Christ's Resurrection that all turned!.

And it does still, of course! Paul is clear about this, and insistent. To friends of his in Corinth, he puts it in a letter: "*If Christ be not risen, then is our preaching vain, and your faith is also vain*" (1 Corinthians 15:14; A.V.).

*

After three days! And even as He said,
    Lo, with the rising morn He rose again.
After three days – and with Him from the dead,
    Hope rose immortal, in the hearts of men.

And to this day it is a joy to report how meaningful this is to Christians everywhere, from the highest to the lowliest. When Professor A. M. Hunter wrote a book he titled *The Work and Word of Jesus*, he sent a copy of it, at her request, to Her Royal Majesty the Queen – now our loved Queen Mother. (The last chapter of that book centres on the Resurrection.) After taking time enough to read it, that gracious lady sent a letter to the author saying how much she had enjoyed it, and also confessing: "I am sorry to say, I read the last chapter first, which is, I know, dreadful cheating: but it makes a wonderful and hopeful background to the rest of the book, and I do not regret it. *Perhaps the light of the Resurrection will yet flood the world!*"

That is a fine expression of faith! And in our life here we cannot do without it – we must, as Paul urged his Corinthian friends, *build everything upon it*! Neville Talbot was someone who, in our day, did that. Serving as a young soldier, the years made him President of the Oxford Union, then Chaplain of Balliol College, and in time Bishop of Pretoria. He was a man of fine physique and spirituality, along with gifts of the mind – and widely loved. He married lovely Cecil Mary Eastwood and he, and all his friends, knew himself to be richly blessed.

Then suddenly, with the birth of their second child, the young wife and mother died. But in that dark hour, Neville Talbot found himself mightily supported, as many another has been, grasping, in the realest sense possible in this earth-life, the certainty of *Christ's Resurrection*. And he cabled home these clear, simple words: "Darling Cecil died . . . Baby well . . . *Christ is risen!*"

Simple? No, but clear – and gloriously significant!

From the beginning there was no doubt about it. Those men who supported our Lord in His ministry on earth were utterly cast down at His death. Some, like Thomas, needed to be alone in their grief; others, seeking the support of their fellow disciples, shut themselves up apart from their usual life "for fear of the Jews". Others, like Mary and the women friends who accompanied her to His tomb, till the time came for the Resurrection, spent the deadly, dragging hours in between preparing spices to take there. Then, the most tremendous thing in the whole world happened – for them, and for us, too, and nothing has ever been the same since. It was the Resurrection of Jesus from the dead, having conquered sin and Death, to be alive for ever more! Mary saw Him!

There will always be room for varying explanations of *how* it happened, but never any doubt, among those closest, that it did happen. They were men and women completely made-over – transformed, *with a new kind of courage and certainty and living wonder*! And they began at once, to those most involved and in the hardest places, to witness to it! Countless others joined them, then and later. Paul wrote of it triumphantly: "He was seen of

Cephas, then of the twelve; after that, He was seen of about five hundred brethren at once – of whom the greater part remain unto this present, but some are fallen asleep. After that He was seen of James, then of all the apostles. And last of all, He was seen of me also, as one born out of due season" (1 Corinthians 15:5–8; A.V.).

On the Resurrection, the Christian Church in the world was founded. Soon it would honour the *first* day of the week as "The Lord's Day", celebrating the completion of man's Redemption, rather than the *seventh*, the completion of Creation.

For myself, I am unhesitatingly one with those disciples, and with modern-day disciples of whom there are a great many. I will name but two of them in my day: Bishops John Robinson and Hugh Montefiore, in their statement during a public discussion in Great St Mary's in Cambridge. "The empty tomb appears in all four Gospels . . . The Living Christ is the foundation of the Christian Faith!"

In the purposes of God, Mary, a faithful, loving woman, was the first on this earth to see our Risen Lord. Peter and John and the rest of the disciples soon shared the glorious news. There was no holding back. So once I wrote of it with wonder:

> They told it,
> not in some safe, distant place
> where nobody had yet heard –
> but in that very city
> where men had shouted hoarsely,
> "Crucify Him! Crucify Him!"

> They told it,
> not after weeks, years,
> when passions had cooled –
> but at once, within Pilate's hearing,
> and of all who judged, soldiered, shouted,
> involved in that dastardly deed.

Good Company

They told it,
confidently believing –
ran, meeting their Living Lord in the way –
a personal confrontation
that more than an empty Tomb reported,
changed the world!

They told it,
who had scattered in fear,
guilty of denial at a servant's word,
hiding behind shut doors,
sharing stuttering doubt –
transformed now marvellously,
men of mighty courage!

(R.F.S.)

Hospitality

My good friend Cedric has never been one to waste words, even when excited. And he was excited today. I sensed it immediately, as he stepped down from the plane, and came forward to be welcomed. He was home – and that was good! When we could speak to each other, I asked him what had been the highlight of his weeks in Palestine. He answered me but one word: "Hospitality!" And it did not in the least surprise me, for I myself had experienced the reality of that beautiful word in that little land. For me it began in a special way at St Andrew's Hospice in Jerusalem, immediately I got through the hated barbed wire and officialdom of the Mandelbaum Gate. The only check-point in the Israeli-Jordan frontier at last behind me, and with my duplicate passports and travel tickets safely stuffed away in my sling-bag, I was in the hands of friends.

As we sat at ease, talking after meals, they had no more need to edit their every word than had I, and that was a very sustaining relief. And when, after some days, it was time for me to move on, friends of these friends received me, all the way to the Hospice beside the sea of Galilee, and back. In one or two bedrooms and sitting-rooms, I found copies of my books, and this persuaded me immediately that in the things of the heart, we spoke the same language.

Hospitality, I knew from what I had read, had long been a characteristic of that little land. Our Master, of course, had been received as guest in many homes – many more, I feel sure, than those we are told of. Certainly there was the Bethany home of Martha, Mary and Lazarus, that spelled welcome again and again. And Peter the fisherman's little home near the lake-shore is mentioned, especially that time when his "wife's mother was taken with a fever" (Luke 4:38; A.V.). That was an occasion of the sort that Dr Luke liked to record. As a doctor, he was pleased to tell of the healing powers of his Master, and the relief and joy of those in that little home when they saw her on her feet again, ready to serve. It was so wonderful!

A further visit – in contrast, to a lordly home – Dr Luke enjoyed recording, one feels, every bit as much. And again it centred round sickness, and family relief. "Jairus," Dr Luke tells us, "a ruler of the synagogue, fell down at Jesus' feet, and besought Him that *He would come into his house*." And He did! (Luke 8:41–42; A.V.) And again, the issue was a happy one! The restoration of the little twelve-year-old daughter of the family must have given them all joy! And Dr Luke must have seen the practical understanding of his Master, and acknowledgement of the little girl's total renewal, in His considerate request: "Give her something to eat" (Mark 5:43). But I wonder why he didn't report it?

*

But – missing no least detail – he did report the wonderful story of hospitality towards the end of his Gospel, a story that will never fade. We owe to it the vitality of one of our best-loved hymns, but more than that too. It declares that even the Master's death and rising again, *make no difference to His readiness to be guest in homes and hearts, where He feels Himself welcome*!

This time, Dr Luke is able to give us a name, but of only one of the two who showed Him simple hospitality, and that was Cleopas. Perhaps it was his home; but we can't be sure. We don't even know whether he was young or old, or what his occupation was. (It could be, that at heart these things do not really matter.)

At any rate, they had both been away for some days, up in the great city of Jerusalem, a good step from Emmaus (Luke 24:13–35). We first meet them when they are at the point of setting off back. They were neither of them disciples of Jesus in the official sense, but when, during their brief stay in the city, He was roughly taken, falsely judged, and crucified, they knew themselves involved. Stunned, the stark and awful happenings threw them in upon themselves, saying to each other, "Well, it's all over now!" The city, swelled with outsiders, was all of a stir. They might just as well go home.

Who would have thought that it would have come to this? They felt bruised and baffled – and all so suddenly! It was hard to think properly in such a crowd. Only one thing surfaced in their muddled minds: they must have been mistaken, for they had really put their faith in that Young Man! There was just time to get home by dusk, if they set off right away. So, tired and thwarted, they set off, through the nearest city gate, heads down, walking together silently, at first.

But they couldn't keep from turning it over. There was this happening that they wanted to discuss – and that – and that!

And after a time – how long a time, there was no telling – they were joined by another. They didn't know Him, but when He could see that a word from Him wouldn't be resented, He found Himself asking: "What manner of communications are these that ye have one to another, as ye walk, and are sad? And the one of them, whose name was Cleopas, answering said unto him, Art thou only a stranger in Jerusalem, and hast not known the things which are come to pass there in these days? And he said unto them, What things? And they said unto him, Concerning Jesus of Nazareth, which was a prophet mighty in deed and word before God and all the people: and how the chief priests and our rulers delivered him to be condemned to death, and have crucified him. But we trusted that it had been He which should have redeemed Israel: and beside all this, today is the third day since these things were done. Yea [they added, their words now tumbling out], and certain women also of our company made us astonished, which were early at the sepulchre; and when they found not his body, they came, saying, that they had also seen a vision of angels, which said that he was alive. And certain of them which were with us went to the sepulchre, and found it even so as the women had said: but him they saw not." Who could wonder that they were grieved and puzzled?

Then, to their surprise, the next words came from the stranger who had joined them on the road: "O fools, and slow of heart to believe all that the prophets have spoken: ought not Christ to have suffered these things, and to enter into his glory? And, beginning at Moses and all the prophets, he expounded unto them in all the scriptures the things concerning himself.

"And they drew nigh unto the village, whither they went [their shadows now long in the roadway], and he made as though he would have gone further. But they constrained him, saying, Abide with us: for it is towards evening, and the day is far spent. [In a little while, they all knew, it would quite suddenly be dark.] And he went in to tarry with them."

Was there a little bustle at first, I wonder, as they collected their wits for practical things of the moment, after a few days away? Anyhow, they found something to eat. "And it came to pass, as he sat at meat with them [to return to Dr Luke's words], he took bread, and blessed it, and brake, and gave to them." A little unusual, they must have thought, He at the head! And what was there familiar about those hands, as He raised them in blessing? And what were those marks? they wondered. And hardly daring to breathe their thoughts, next moment they knew. He was no mere traveller interested in their troubles; no mere Rabbi wonderfully learned in the scriptures; no weary guest – *but their Lord*!

And soon, wasting no time, they were eagerly on their way back to others who loved Him, sharing their confusion and grief, in the city. But they had something new to say. They told of their walk to Emmaus, adding: "Did not our heart burn within us, while he talked with us by the way, and while he opened to us the scriptures? . . . And they told what things were done in the way [and how He had entered their modest homes as Guest], and how he was known of them in breaking of bread!"

So it was true: He was alive!

A marvellous discovery, and Luke never wrote down a greater story, or one more real!

In an effort to express its wonder today, one of our poets has written:

> Shakespeare is dust, and will not come
> To question from his Avon tomb,
> And Socrates and Shelley keep
> An Attic and Italian sleep . . .
>
> They see not. But, O Christians, who
> Throng Holborn and Fifth Avenue,
> May you not meet, in spite of death,
> A traveller from Nazareth?
>
> (Drinkwater)

There are many of us who can confidently say, you may! And sometimes, in the direst circumstances – walking your own Emmaus Road – you can be overtaken by One gloriously alive, having conquered Death, and invite Him across the secret threshold of your life. Nurse Edith Cavell was one who knew the wonder of this experience, and I was reminded of her witness to it, as I stood one day, with her two sisters, on a little patch of green, where caring hearts had placed small crosses in remembrance, outside Westminster Abbey. That courageous English nurse was one who strengthened my Christian faith greatly.

Seized by military spies, and marched through darkened streets to the silence of an enemy prison, her grasp of the central reality of her Risen Lord never wavered. After an exacting period, the day came when she had perforce to stand trial. She stood unafraid, wearing her spotless uniform, and on her arm the badge of mercy. But there was no mercy for her; she made her appeal as to hearts of stone, and was returned to her cell. In that little cell – before she was finally led forth, with bandaged eyes, to her martyrdom – she took from the hands of her chaplain the symbols of the Holy Sacrament, and repeated with a calm and beautiful confidence words from that hymn known by many believing hearts worldwide: "*Abide with me!*" Written by the beloved Henry Francis Lyte, ministering in Brixham, Devon, its words expressed the faith that held her:

> I need Thy presence every passing hour,
> What but Thy grace can foil the tempter's power?
> Who, like Thyself, my guide and stay can be?
> Through cloud and sunshine, O abide with me.

And countless times, that prayer-hymn, uttered by a humble heart seeking the Divine Guest, has proved sufficient! As to that ministering Englishwoman in the little time left to her:

> I fear no foe, with Thee at hand to bless;
> Ills have no weight, and tears no bitterness;
> Where is death's sting? Where, grave, thy victory?
> *I triumph still, if Thou abide with me.*

Witnesses Wanted

My neighbour Peter had some news for me today, as we joined the bus out of the city. He'd been called to the Court, not as an offender, fortunately, but as a witness, though that had been unwelcome enough. If you yourself have had that experience, you will know something of how it struck Peter.

I chose not to mention the fact that I loved the word "witness", that I felt certain was one of Dr Luke's favourite words, but in any case, the bus came just then. However, some day I shall speak of it, when Peter is further away from this day's experience.

The whole of the thrilling story of the Book of Acts, of course, turns on that word "witness". Dr Luke has hardly started when that becomes certain. His two books have this understandable link, one being about "all that Jesus *began* both to do and to teach" (Acts 1:1; A.V.), and his new book – "The Acts of the Apostles" – being about what He gloriously *continued* to do *through His witnesses*. And Dr Luke, as eager as ever with his writing, starts immediately with that pivotal word of his Risen Lord and Master (Acts 1:8; A.V.). He was commissioning His followers: and one gets the feeling that there is no time to lose. They have so much to share, beginning just where they are. But not staying there! His words are: "Ye shall be *witnesses unto Me* both in Jerusalem, and in all Judaea, and in Samaria, and unto the uttermost parts of the earth." A thrilling programme!

"Our problem", said the world-embracing Dr William Barclay, after giving us that word "witness" in Greek, "is that the word, for us, tends to be connected with legal evidence in a court of law." This, of course, limits it, and

causes it to lose its experience of wonder and joy.
Beginning just where they were, in Jerusalem, the Risen
Lord's great plan was that His dedicated "witnesses"
should operate in ever-extending concentric circles – out
from Jerusalem to the next place, Judaea, and out again to
Samaria, the semi-Jewish state which would be a kind of
bridge towards the heathen world, and so out to the
uttermost parts of the earth. (Palestine was a little country,
only a hundred and twenty miles long, and a mere forty
wide. It simply couldn't be made to contain all that was
involved in His Gospel!)

As this word fell on the ears of those involved, both men
and women, after the Resurrection, it must have led them
to straighten up, and with all their faculties alert, know
seriously all that it could cost them: for the Greek word for
witness and the word for *martyr* were, they knew, one and
the same: *martus*.

But in a short time they were joined by other followers
– as their Lord intended should be the case. Religion was
more than a refuge to the individual human spirit; it had
never been that to Jesus, throughout the whole of His
experience on earth. And now He was sending out, with
hurrying feet, those who were ready to follow Him. To be
a *witness* was to know something larger than security: the
spiritual realization of their Lord's living nearness. And
that, they discovered, was gloriously sufficient. There was
no promise of an escape from hazards, but there was no
doubt about the Spirit in which this campaign was
launched!

In time, Dr Luke was setting down his record. Later, in
opening as strikingly as always what is now the seventeenth
chapter of his Book of Acts, he set out to tell what he
wanted to share. He said: "Travelling on through
Amphipolis and Apollonia, they [Paul and Silas] reached
Thessalonica" (Moffatt). It sounds like a peaceful saunter;
but it was nothing of the sort. There waited for them no
welcoming speeches, but rather a continuation of what had

happened in other places. They witnessed to Jesus the Messiah, Who had suffered, died, and risen from the dead. "Some", he found words to say, "were persuaded and threw in their lot with Paul and Silas, including a host of devout Greeks, and a large number of the leading women." (That was fine – but it was not all!)

His next verse, perforce, goes on: "But the Jews were roused to jealousy; they got hold of some idle rascals to form a mob and set the town in an uproar." And what of Paul and Silas? Some citizens had only one thing to say, and that with anger, yelling: "*These upsetters of the whole world have come here too*" (vv. 1–7, Moffatt's Version).

*

But Dr Luke must have known of countless other witnesses, when he was writing his book "The Acts of the Apostles". The names and deeds of many of them have come down to us. Paul made room for a good list in his own "Epistle to the Romans", in what we now treasure as chapter 16. And it pleases me that Paul starts off, as he does: "Let me introduce our sister Phoebe, a deaconess of the church at Cenchreae", and goes on to a home-making couple, "Prisca and Aquila, my fellow-workers in Christ Jesus, who have risked their lives for me" (v. 3, Moffatt's Version). And I'm greatly tempted to go on – but the list is so long, of many people whose names don't appear anywhere else. Several of the names are linked with those of "the church that meets in their house" – and this was a daring thing to do in those early days! And here, linked together as "witnesses", are Tryphaena and Tryphosa. (Are they also husband and wife? I must look them up. No, Dr Hastings thinks more likely sisters, or near relations of some kind. Well, it's fitting that they should be remembered, for many such people through the centuries have been wonderful witnesses.) And Urbanus is remembered – a common name for a slave, or a servant, in the early days of the Church. And it's nice to have him remembered too, for many servants up through the centuries have been good witnesses to Christ. And don't miss "that choice Christian, Rufus", as Paul calls him; for we, too, have known many choice Christian witnesses. But there are so many; take down your New Testament, ponder their names, and try to imagine what life was like to them. For they were witnesses to our common Lord in their day – as you and I are in ours, here and now. And it will be borne in upon you that we belong to a courageous, glorious, and gracious company!

"In the first hundred years after the New Testament was written", says Dr James Reid to us, "there is no record of a single outstanding preacher. But Christianity was spread by ordinary people, telling the story of the love of Christ to those whom they met in the circle of their friends." And that, had we a Paul or a Dr Luke to write their names down for us, could have been the story of every century till now. *Do we belong to that company, today?*

Then let us see to it that the same kind of loyalty and reality continues. Nothing must be allowed to mock our witness. It is too important. When Sir Winston Churchill was called to inspect a particular naval set-up during the war, we are told, officials took him out to see fighting ships, formidable looking, anchored off-shore. They had told him that they were really "dummies", "decoys" without a single weapon aboard, intended to mislead the enemy's reconnaissance planes, and had been made of lath-and-plaster, cork and plywood. They might have served their purpose, but they didn't, and couldn't. Why?

"Well," the great man looked at them, and then said to the pained naval chief and officers who stood waiting, "they won't fool anybody for long."

"Why, sir?" they asked.

"*No seagulls!*" said he.

Then it dawned upon them, that their pretence really was "phoney", and they stood aghast, seeing what they hadn't seen before: that there is something wrong with a

ship, teeming with hungry, hard-serving men, that has no
refuse to throw over the side into the harbour at set times.
(After that, men were detailed to go out daily, and attend
to the matter!)

Unreality soon betrays itself. *And it can, of course, even
in our Christian witness!* You can call some of those early
Christians naïve if you like – but they knew that much, and
more.

Christian witnessing is not acting a part, but living a life,
here and now. It is not standing around looking pious,
meekly adjusting one's halo – not at all. That life has
sometimes to be lived where it is strenuous, dull, or
difficult. And being persons of this age, our *witness* has to
be presented in a way that will meet modern minds with a
ring of reality. Words of witness there must be: *but words
without works are empty: as works without words are dumb!*

We must each offer a lively witness, in our own way. Said
one to another who did this:

> Not merely in the words you say,
>   Not only in your deeds confessed,
> But in the most unconscious way
>   Is Christ expressed.
>
> Is it a beatific smile?
>   A holy light upon your brow?
> Oh, no! I felt His presence while
>   You laughed just now.
>
> For me 'twas not the truth you taught,
>   To you so clear, to me so dim,
> But when you came to me you brought
>   A sense of Him.
>
> And from your eyes He beckons me,
>   And from your heart His love is shed,
> Till I lose sight of you – and see
>   The Christ instead.
>
> (Unknown)

Loyal Doctor Luke

I have been constantly called on to speak of some good book I have discovered, and I count that high among this life's delights. It makes no difference whether I have chanced on it in my public library, or bought it for my own shelves. It's not hard to understand how the enormous number of books published nowadays – good, dull or rubbishy – confuses many would-be readers. That has been true for a long time, and is more than ever true today. An American once asked Dr Denney of Glasgow whether he could recommend a good Life of Christ. The old saint answered: "*Have you read the one that Luke wrote?*"

It was a proper question, and a bright one, for there is no other account quite like it. But, of course, there are two: the first, "what Jesus *began* to do and teach, until the day when He was taken up . . .", and the second follows, as to what *He continued to do* after that time through His Spirit, energizing those He had chosen for the thrilling world task of establishing His Church.

How long Dr Luke gave up time to his writing there is no telling, only that he seems to have given every possible care to make his twofold record as worthy as possible of the amazing story he had to tell. Its human and divine elements are seen to combine. His writing races along with exciting verve; it is crowded with people – and there is nothing stuffily pious about it. Men and women, both have a complementary place there – although this was not always the case in records of those early times. In Palestine and adjoining countries, a woman was all too often regarded as merely a thing, with no legal rights whatsoever, much less opportunities in public life. But this was a different kind of story: the power of Jesus's personal mastery, where it was accepted, changed things!

And modern-day scholars are as eager to tell us how good Luke's Greek was, his words strikingly and carefully chosen! And he was equally at pains to check his facts as his story unfolded. He was, of course, writing in very early days, when many whose experiences were being recorded by his graphic pen were still alive.

More than this – when he set down what now comes to us in our English New Testament, translated from his careful Greek, as Acts, chapter 15, going on into 16, he is suddenly seen to take on an autobiographical turn. It is clear to us, his readers, that he was present – *he is using the term "we", as one involved*. This form of writing appears first in Acts 16:10, after he has told of the dream-like call his friend Paul received, from a man in Macedonia, saying: "Come over . . . and help us!" "And after he had seen the vision," are the exact words of Dr Luke, "immediately *we* endeavoured to go into Macedonia, assuredly gathering that the Lord had called *us* to preach the Gospel unto them." The crisp way he sets it down, gives anyone reading it the feeling that he was moved to be involved in that exciting project with Paul his friend – and not only that he would be able to look after his health (never really robust) on what would undoubtedly turn out to be a strenuous undertaking. His spirit is, as it were, on tiptoe! He doesn't take a week of days to think about it, or call in a church committee to give it exhaustive consideration – the word he uses in telling of it, translates into our lovely word of response "immediately"! And on he goes (vv. 11–12): "Therefore loosing from Troas, we came with a *straight course* to Samothracia, and the next day to Neapolis; and from thence to Philippi, which is the chief city of that part of Macedonia . . ." These are men on the job; there is no delay – one can almost see their faces shining with expectation!

"And on the sabbath", Luke goes on, "*we* went out of the city by the river side, where prayer was wont to be

made; and *we* sat down, and spake unto the women which
resorted thither.'' (They didn't stop to think it beneath
their dignity – just women! No distinguished church leaders
in their best academic and preaching gowns out to meet
them, having come so promptly, and so far. Just women!)

But there was one, at any rate, they were later to
discover, whom Luke would be glad to name in his record.
''A certain woman named Lydia,'' he says, ''a seller of
purple, of the city of Thyatira [a business woman], which
worshipped God, heard *us*; whose heart the Lord opened
that she attended unto the things which were spoken of
Paul. And when she was baptized, and her household, she
besought *us*, saying, 'If ye have judged me to be faithful to
the Lord, come into my house, and abide there.' And she
constrained us'', Luke must have been pleased to say – for
this fine expression of Christian hospitality was something
to be welcomed, something more than they had expected
for travel in Europe was very hard in those days!

Lydia, as a business woman, would be used to organizing
things, no doubt, and she would have house servants, a
well as those employed in her business. ''The purple dye
in which she dealt,'' Dr Barclay tells us, ''was so costly that
a pound of wool dyed with it could cost as much as the
equivalent of £40. It had to be gathered, drop by drop
from a certain shellfish.'' She would live in a good house
but it was her good hospitality of spirit that impressed Dr
Luke, it seems certain. She would make her guests – these
missionaries till lately unknown, often weary, always
wandering – very comfortable for the brief time they could
be together. And no one better deserved to share that
memorable experience. (It holds its place among all the
''*We*'' passages in Luke's Book of Acts: chapters 20:5–16
21:1–18; 27:1–29, for instance.)

*

And as we read the lines – and between the lines – of that
lively book we now call ''The Acts of the Apostles'', we see

revealed for our encouragement the lovely spirit of Dr Luke himself. Along with his medical skill, and his eagerness to serve, there is no forgetting his glorious *loyalty*. Shown chiefly to Paul, at a time when he specially needed it, Dr Barclay describes it as *"one of the greatest examples of sheer loyalty in the history of the Church"*. And that is saying much! But it helps us to round out the picture we have of Paul's good friend.

Loyalty is a very God-like quality. In one verse (Psalm 36:5; Moffatt's Version), the psalmist uplifts his heart to declare: "Eternal One, Thy love is high as heaven, *Thy loyalty* soars to the very skies!" Then in the Old Testament book of Proverbs (chapter 3:3; Moffatt's Version again), we have this striking injunction: "Never let kindness and *loyalty* go, tie them fast round your neck." And when we come to the New Testament (Romans 16:19; Moffatt), we find Paul writing of this same lovely quality – and what words he chooses to address to his friends in Rome! "Everyone has heard of your *loyalty* to the Gospel; it makes me rejoice over you!"

Dr Luke finds a place in his Book of Acts to tell of Paul's last journey there, as a prisoner. *And the doctor, of his own choice, was still loyally present*. He writes (in what is now Acts 27:1–10, in Moffatt's Version): "When it was decided that *we* were to sail for Italy, Paul and some other prisoners were handed over to an officer of the Imperial regiment . . . Embarking in an Adramyttian ship which was bound for the Asiatic seaports, *we* set sail, accompanied by a Macedonian from Thessalonica called Aristarchus. Next day *we* put in at Sidon . . .

"Putting to sea from there, *we* had to sail under the lee of Cyprus, as the wind was against us; then, sailing over the Cilician and Pamphylian waters, *we* came to Myra in Lycia. There the officer found an Alexandrian ship bound for Italy, and put us on board of her. For a number of days *we* made a slow passage and had *great difficulty* . . ." (And those words are to appear again and again in the record.)

"So Paul warned them . . . 'I see this voyage is going to be attended with hardship and serious loss . . .' However the officer let himself be persuaded by the captain and the owner rather than by anything Paul could say, and as the harbour was badly placed for wintering in, the majority proposed to set sail and try if they could reach Phoenix . . . (Phoenix is a Cretan harbour facing S.W. and N.W.). When a moderate southerly breeze sprang up, they thought they had secured their object, and after weighing anchor they sailed along the coast of Crete, close inshore." (But they are not yet safe, by any means.)

"Presently down rushed a hurricane . . . the ship was caught . . . so *we* gave up and let her drive along. Running under the lee of a small island called Clauda, *we* managed *with great difficulty* . . . they used ropes to undergird the ship, and in fear of being stranded on the Syrtis they lowered the sail and lay to. As *we* were being terribly battered by the storm, they had to jettison the cargo next day, while two days later they threw the ship's gear overboard with their own hands; for many days neither sun nor stars could be seen, the storm raged heavily . . ." (The fury put a frightening strain, not only on the ship, but on the hungry crew. For it was impossible to get food while in such a plight.)

"When the fourteenth night arrived," Luke had still to report, "*we* were drifting about in the sea of Adria, when the sailors about midnight suspected land was near. On taking soundings they found twenty fathoms, and a little further on, when they sounded again, they found fifteen. Then, afraid of being stranded on the rocks, they let go four anchors from the stern and longed for daylight . . . Paul begged them all to take some food. 'For fourteen days,' he said, 'you have been on the watch all the time, without a proper meal. Take some food then, I beg of you; it will keep you alive.' . . .

"Now the soldiers [v. 42] were resolved to kill the prisoners, in case any of them swam off and escaped; but as the officer wanted to save Paul, he put a stop to their plan, ordering those who could swim to jump overboard first and get to land, while the rest were to manage with planks or pieces of wreckage. In this way it 'urned out that the whole company got safe to land." (And they were seventy-six souls, in all!)

Altogether, it was a terribly hazardous undertaking. Paul – in indifferent health, hardly fit to manage his work – must have been worn out by the time it was through. Understandably, Paul was profoundly thankful for Luke's company. And that would be, of course, not only on his voyage to Italy, where he was to be a prisoner in Rome, *but in prison itself.* Sympathetic Christian friends and helpers were kind to Paul there, as he took pleasure in recording in many of his letters, mentioning them by name. But a time came when he had to write: "*Only Luke is with me*" (2 Timothy 4:11; A.V.).

Steady, helpful, *loyal* Luke!

*

And many of us, since then, have had cause to give God thanks for human loyalty. If you are privileged ever to go to Washington Cathedral, note the ninety-six figures on the reredos; and chief among them, just now let me commend the remembrance there of the Chinese Anglican priest, Fung Mei Ts'en. (His name appears again in one of the Te Deum windows of the Cathedral, it is so special.) He was brought up to follow the philosopher Confucius, and it was not until he was in his thirties that he became a Christian in his home town. He had always been very clever, so that when he offered himself as a catechist, his church was delighted. For seven years he continued loyally to teach the faith that now meant so much to him. In 1922 he was ordained, and given charge of St James's Church, Chuho, a city about ninety miles west of Hankow. Of his ministry there, one wrote very tellingly: "His word could always be trusted, and his life was blameless." For all that his salary was meagre, he supported his wife and three sons – one of whom was blind – together with his aged father, and a crippled brother of his, with a wife and two little children. In addition to these family cares he was known to be generous to the poor when he chanced upon them.

In the early morning of an April day in 1930, some two thousand guerrillas of the Red Army surged into the city of Chuho. They killed many leading citizens, looted shops and houses, and finally came to Fung Mei Ts'en's church. "Who is your priest?" they demanded of the many people who had hastened there, seeking refuge, and at that point Fung Mei Ts'en himself stepped forward to say, "I am he."

He was arrested and bundled out of his church, to face what turned out to be a mere pretence of trial. And under sentence of death, carried out a few days later, he was shot on 22nd April 1930. He wrote to his bishop, "I, Mei, have perfect peace in my heart, but Bishop, I want you to think of me as giving my life as a sacrifice for the sake of the Gospel." And so he is remembered, just as, in many places the world around, we remember St Paul, who also gave up his life for the same Gospel, along with *his loyal friend, Dr Luke*!

Loyalty, as most of us know it, is not alone a missionary task at all; it involves God; the church where we worship; the family to which we belong; the firm for which we work; the club where we find our recreational fun – any one of which may sometimes seem a little tedious. To manage *loyalty* at all, we need more than human strength!

> Whoso hath felt the Spirit of the Highest
> Cannot confound nor doubt Him nor deny,
> Yea, with one voice, O world, tho' thou deniest,
> Stand thou on that side, *for on this am I*!

> (Meyer)

Amidst God's Good Company

Gracious Father, I rejoice in what we know of You,
through the framework, and beauty of the world, wherein
You have set us;

    but chiefly, through Your Son, our Saviour, Jesus
        Christ;

    through friendly human eyes of many known to us;

    through the ongoing worship and ministry of Your
        Church.

I bless You, for all high and low, who serve our needy
        fellows;

    through acts of love and neighbourliness;

    through the sharing of knowledge and experience;

    through helpful gifts of money, and hospitality.

I bless You for all who heighten life's values through good
        buildings, and art, and books written, and read,

    through music and song of voice and instrument;

    through refreshment of gardens – and honest laughter.

I bless You for the trust of little children;

    for the adventuresomeness of youth;

    for the steady dependability of many in maturity;

    for rich gifts of toil, and travel shared in old age.

Good Company

Hold in Your kindly keeping today, all who feel themselves
    too frail to take an active part in things;
      may their prayers sustain and strengthen others;
      may their long, good lives inspire and enrich others.

And so bring us all, with unflagging faith, and expectation,
to our sharing in the Larger Life, beyond this earth-
experience. AMEN.

                                (R.F.S.)

Acknowledgements

The author and publisher are grateful for permission to use the following material from other writers in this book:

Joan Bruce, "In overcrowded Bethlehem".

John Drinkwater, "Shakespeare is dust . . ." from his *Collected Poems – Vol. II – 1917–22*, Sidgwick & Jackson, 1923.

Eleanor Farjeon, "There isn't time" from *Silver Sand and Snow*, Michael Joseph, 1951, by kind permission of The Estate of Eleanor Farjeon.

Arthur Feslier, extract from a talk broadcast by the New Zealand Broadcasting Corporation.

John Masefield, "Everlasting Mercy", by kind permission of The Society of Authors as the literary representative of The Estate of John Masefield.

Ernest Raymond, an obituary on Pamela Frankau from the biennial report of the Royal Society of Literature.

Muriel Stuart, "Here in a quiet and dusty room", from *A Book of Town Verse*, chosen by T. W. Sussams, OUP, 1947.

Anne Treneer, *School House in the Wind*, Jonathan Cape, 1950, by kind permission of the Executors of the Anne Treneer Estate.

Painstaking research has failed to locate a few copyright-owners of quotations. The author and publisher offer apologies and, where possible, will right the matter in subsequent editions.

Also available in Fount Paperbacks

BOOKS BY RITA SNOWDEN

Discoveries That Delight

'Thirty brief chapters of reflections on selected psalms . . . The book is very readable. Its style has been achieved through many years of work to produce a vehicle of religious communication with a wide appeal.'

Neville Ward, Church of England Newspaper

Further Good News

'Another enjoyable book from Rita Snowden; easy to read and with a store of good things to ponder over and store in the mind. The author shows clearly that there is much Good News in our world and that this is very much the gift of a loving God.'

Church Army Review

I Believe Here and Now

'Once again she has produced for us one of the most readable and helpful pieces of Christian witness I have seen . . .'

D. P. Munro, Life and Work

A Woman's Book of Prayer

'This book will make prayer more real and meaningful for all who use it. There is all through the book an accent of reality. Here the needs of the twentieth century are brought to God in twentieth century language.'

William Barclay

More Prayers for Women

'. . . she has that rare and valuable gift of being able to compose forms of prayer which really do express the aspirations of many people . . .'

Philip Cecil, Church Times

Also available in Fount Paperbacks

Yours Faithfully – Volume 1
GERALD PRIESTLAND

'There can be no doubt that Gerald Priestland has brought new life to the reporting of religious news. Nothing as good has happened to radio since Alistair Cooke started "Letter from America".'

Edwin Robertson, Baptist Times

Yours Faithfully – Volume 2
GERALD PRIESTLAND

'He is positive, informed, urbane, incisive, witty and unafraid. His speech is always with grace seasoned with salt . . .'

W. M. Macartney, Life and Work

Gerald Priestland at Large
GERALD PRIESTLAND

'This final collection of *Yours Faithfully* broadcast talks . . . is as apposite as it is humane and humorous . . . Gerald Priestland's usually wise and thoughtful opinions make this book a very good buy.'

Mary Endersbee, Today

Also available in Fount Paperbacks

BOOKS BY WILLIAM BARCLAY

The Plain Man's Book of Prayers

'A treasure indeed . . . it bears throughout Professor Barclay's magnificent combination of lucidity and depth.'

British Weekly

More Prayers for the Plain Man

'*The Plain Man's Book of Prayers* has had a wonderful reception . . . Professor Barclay has a genius for sensing what the public will take . . .'

Church Times

Prayers for Help and Healing

'A masterpiece of common sense and well-balanced thinking about the whole perplexing problem of human disease and its cure.'

J. B. Phillips

The New Testament

'We can only commend, with admiration and astonishment, this further instance of Professor Barclay's twofold expertise – in the whole area of New Testament studies and in the needs of Christian readers today.'

Expository Times

Fount Paperbacks

Fount is one of the leading paperback publishers of religious books and below are some of its recent titles.

- ☐ THE QUIET HEART George Appleton £2.95
- ☐ PRAYER FOR ALL TIMES Pierre Charles £1.75
- ☐ SEEKING GOD Esther de Waal £1.75
- ☐ THE SCARLET AND THE BLACK
  J. P. Gallagher £1.75
- ☐ TELL MY PEOPLE I LOVE THEM
  Clifford Hill £1.50
- ☐ CONVERSATIONS WITH THE CRUCIFIED
  Reid Isaac £1.50
- ☐ THE LITTLE BOOK OF SYLVANUS
  David Kossoff £1.50
- ☐ DOES GOD EXIST? Hans Küng £5.95
- ☐ GEORGE MACDONALD: AN ANTHOLOGY
  George MacDonald C. S. Lewis (ed.) £1.50
- ☐ WHY I AM STILL A CATHOLIC
  Robert Nowell (ed.) £1.50
- ☐ THE GOSPEL FROM OUTER SPACE
  Robert L. Short £1.50
- ☐ CONTINUALLY AWARE Rita Snowden £1.75
- ☐ TRUE RESURRECTION Harry Williams £1.75
- ☐ WHO WILL DELIVER US? Paul Zahl £1.50

All Fount paperbacks are available at your bookshop or newsagent, or they can also be ordered by post from Fount Paperbacks, Cash Sales Department, G.P.O. Box 29, Douglas, Isle of Man, British Isles. Please send purchase price, plus 15p per book, maximum postage £3. Customers outside the U.K. send purchase price, plus 15p per book. Cheque, postal or money order. No currency.

NAME (Block letters) _____

ADDRESS _____

_____

_____

While every effort is made to keep prices low, it is sometimes necessary to increase them at short notice. Fount Paperbacks reserve the right to show new retail prices on covers which may differ from those previously advertised in the text or elsewhere.